JESUS, THE STRANGER

JESUS, THE STRANGER

Reflections on the Gospels

Joseph G. Donders

ORBIS BOOKS

Maryknoll, New York 10545

The Catholic Foreign Mission Society of America (Maryknoll) recruits and trains people for overseas missionary service. Through Orbis Books Maryknoll aims to foster the international dialogue which is essential to mission. The books published, however, reflect the opinions of their authors and are not meant to represent the official position of the Society.

Sermons 8, 9, 10, 18, 23, 24, 26, 27, 31, 32, 35, 37, and 52 were first published as *Expatriate Jesus* (Nairobi: Gazelle Books, 1975).

Copyright © 1978 by Orbis Books, Maryknoll, NY 10545

Printed in the United States of America

Library of Congress Cataloging in Publication Data
Donders, Joseph G
  Jesus, the stranger.

  1. Catholic Church—Sermons. 2. Sermons, English.
I. Title.
BX1756.D634J47   252'.02   77-21783
ISBN 0-88344-234-5
ISBN 0-88344-235-3 pbk.

CONTENTS

INTRODUCTION

This is a book of sermons.
Sermons that were made and given in the heart of Africa.
Sermons that were attended by as many Kenyan students
as their Saint Paul's Catholic University Chapel can hold,
hundreds and hundreds of them.
The community does not consist only of students,
there are professors and lecturers,
administrators and cooks.
And as Nairobi is one of the main African diplomatic centers,
there were representatives from all nations in the world,
especially during the innumerable international conferences
that are held in Nairobi,
successfully and unsuccessfully,
WCC, UNCTAD IV, and so many others.
The composition of the listeners
reflects that prayer in Canon III,
that says that HE, the LORD,
gathers his people from East to West,
and though not mentioned in that prayer,
from North to South as well.
> Sermons are not made only by the preacher.
> If sermons are made only by the preacher,
> then they are not sermons,
> but private and rather personal meditations.
> A type of meditation that is not always
> relevant to the listeners,
> and therefore more often than not boring and dull.
> Real sermons are made by the listeners.
> These sermons are surely made by them.
Without all those students and all those others,
> discussing and arguing,
> believing and disbelieving,

      hoping and despairing,
      finding and losing,
      asking and answering,
      confessing and praying,
      weeping and enjoying,
      worrying and trusting,
      agreeing and protesting,
      planning and plotting,
      opening and blocking,
      singing and drumming,
      blessing and cursing,
      giving up and expecting,
      new and old,
      modern and traditional,
      dogmatic and doubting,
      but all gathering around that man from Nazareth,
      JESUS,
      these sermons would never have been
      what they are in this book,
      neither in their content,
      nor in their form.
They are,
whatever the reader will think of them,
however the reader will judge them,
definitely the result
of the liturgical life,
of the liturgical happenings,
in that chapel in the center of Africa,
in that town.
that even during rainy days,
very proudly calls itself,
THE CITY IN THE SUN.
      We hope that the reader,
      will be able to pick up its rhythm,
      to share this our life,
      coming from that only valid life-giver,
      JESUS CHRIST,
      the Lord of us all.

Part I

BEGINNING

1.

THREE WISE MEN

Three people came from very far
to see Jesus.
In my country
they are traditionally called kings.
In English-speaking countries
they are more often than not
called wise men.
I prefer the title wise men.
I do not know exactly what to do with kings.
I like to see them as wise.
And I think they were wise,
very wise.
  They were obviously seekers.
  And that
  according to many reliable sources
  is the beginning of wisdom.
  They saw a star.
  You might say
  that is not particularly wise,
  everybody can see stars,
  and that is true.
  But to see stars
  you must look up,
  and not everybody looks up.
  When did you see your last star?
  When did you look up last?
  They did not only see that star,
  they saw through that star
  a message.

3

They saw the star
as a sign,
and that means
that they were not only living
in the direct world around them,
like animals do
or insects,
who seem to think only
about food, drink, and sex.
They believed in a beyond,
in a double-up,
in a world behind this world,
in a world different from this world,
    and yet appearing through it.
And that is very wise too.
They did not believe their eyes,
they could not believe
that what they saw
was all there is.
They believed that there is more
to it all.
    They were religious people.
    Non-religious people only believe their eyes.
    Religious people do not
    and cannot only believe their eyes;
    what they see presents itself
    as a further question mark.
Those three
saw that star
as a big beckoning question mark.
It invited them
to somewhere,
and they followed it.
That was another wise move
to follow that star.
    Why did they follow the star?
    I do not know exactly.
    But they must have had

some hope
or some expectation
that something new was going to happen
to this world,
that the past and sin and guilt
were going to be taken away
or at least taken over.
I think
that within the context
in which they appear
we might suppose something like that.
So they were looking for something
which some of us
call nowadays
salvation.
　Looking for that salvation,
　they made another
　very wise decision.
　When they followed the star,
　they were convinced,
　and that is sure,
　because according to the reports
　they themselves said so,
　that they were looking
　　　not for a learned book
　　　that might have the solution;
　　　not for a political system
　　　that might bring liberation to all;
　　　not for a social,
　　　or should we say
　　　sociological theory
　　　that might explain human behavior in such a way
　　　that it might be changed;
　　　not for a psychological gadget
　　　that might help to psychoanalyze
　　　the whole of humankind;
　　　　not at all,
　　　　what they were looking for

was a person.
They were looking for a child.
And that was very, very wise,
because if you come to think of it,
salvation can come only
from a person.
  I will explain
  why I think so.
    Take Jesus.
    At a certain moment
    he is telling the parable
    of the prodigal son,
    about that father
    willing to forgive.
    That is a very nice story,
    a classic
    without any doubt.
    Even its economy of words
    is absolutely remarkable.
    But that whole story
    does not help us a stitch,
    except in the case
    that the teller of that story
    can assure us,
    that that Father,
    that God the Father
    he seemed to talk about,
    is a real person
    willing to take that type
    of personal attitude.
We know the same thing
when we go to a hospital.
The hospital is full
of the most wonderful intensive care and other units,
full of pacemakers, iron lungs,
artificial kidney rinsers,
and who knows what.

We know that all that
is NOTHING
if there is no PERSON
willing to mediate
between all those machines
and me.
If there is no personal interest
in me
it is all useless.
    And in a school it is the same;
    all the books,
    all the teaching aids are there,
    but it is the personnel
    that makes the school,
    or breaks it.
A neglected child
is not helped
by a report,
by a plan,
or by a building.
The child is helped
by a hand
and a voice
that says:
    I,
    I am going to help you.
Those three wise men
knew that.
They wanted liberation;
they were looking for an assurance
from the other side;
they were looking
for a hand
and
for a voice.
    The hand and the voice
    of God,

and they found it,
and they went home other men,
they went home even via another way.
If we think about it,
we are in the same position.
We are in their position.
We are looking for several things,
I am looking for several things,
I am suffering under a guilty conscience,
dishonest,
unfair,
overlooking,
refusing,
I feel that my hands are dirty,
after so long in this world,
and I would like
an assurance that all this
can be restored and forgiven,
or even better forgotten.
I am looking for a new life,
for another type of possibilities,
for a greater integrity.
And to be able to find all that,
we do not need a system,
a moral code,
a theory,
a theology,
a policy,
a philosophy,
or something like that.
We need
a person.
We need Jesus.

2.

JOHN THE BAPTIST, AN OLD-TIMER

People wondered about Saint John the Baptist.
And they had very good reasons to be surprised:
    He came from the desert,
    he did not work,
    he did not own anything,
    he did not eat bread
    made by human hands,
    he did not drink wine
    pressed from grapes;
    he ate nature as it fell from God's hands:
    grasshoppers,
    locusts,
    snails,
    and honey.
    He did not use an inch of textile;
    he was dressed in a camel's skin,
    with a leather girdle
    made of another skin.
And his teaching,
his teaching was remarkable too.
It was so remarkable,
because it was so hard-hitting,
and so one-sided.
    He called his public,
    people who after all
    showed sufficient good will
    to come to be converted:

a brood of snakes,
and he announced
without any further hesitation
that as far as he was concerned
God's judgment was very near
and that everybody would be cut down
like a tree
and thrown in the fire,
in a fire that never would go out.
He maintained
that everybody should convert;
he said that everybody
should be baptized by him;
he said that everybody
should change their life,
and quickly,
without hesitation:
policemen,
soldiers,
and housewives.
He was not so clear
on what would happen
to those who would convert.
He was more outspoken
and very clear
on what would happen
to those who would not convert.
The future,
John pointed out,
was God's wrath,
his anger,
his vengeance,
and fury.
He did not exclude the possibility of being saved,
otherwise he would not have asked people to be baptized,
but he does not dwell on that theme very much.
His message is somber
and grim

and dark
and heavy.
Jesus himself would compare,
afterwards,
John's approach
and the song he was singing
with a funeral song,
a dirge,
something belonging to last rites.
And Jesus blamed,
afterwards,
the Jews
for not having understood,
for not having wept.

Jesus himself did understand,
Jesus did weep,
and he went up to John
to be baptized.
John got frightened;
he said: No, not you by me;
but Jesus said: Oh, yes, me by you.
And he was baptized,
to show that he shared the feelings,
the prophetic inspiration,
and the prophetic impulse
of Saint John.
John was right.
Jesus sealed his opinion.
But John was right in the old way.
John was right according to the Old Testament pattern.
But with Saint John that Old Testament closed.
Something else came instead,
somebody else had come to replace it.
John's message was a message of Doom;
not only that,
but mainly that.
It hardly could be called: "Good News."
After John this changes;

it changed while John baptized Jesus
and when the Spirit descended upon him
in a way it never descended upon earth before
to start something new,
a new era,
a new period.
    An era in which
        a father was looking for a lost son,
        a shepherd for his lost sheep,
        a host for his reluctant guests,
        and Jesus for all those who are sick
        and sinful.
Jesus himself made that difference very clear.
He spoke about a complete break.
He said:
    Up to the time of John
    it was the law and the prophets;
    since him
    it is the kingdom of God.
Saint John lamented,
Jesus rejoiced.
John sang a funeral hymn,
Jesus an alleluia verse.
John refused to eat bread,
Jesus broke his bread.
John refused to drink wine,
Jesus turned all the water in the kitchen into wine.
John walked in a camel's skin,
Jesus in a shirt without seam.
John warned,
Jesus invited.
They were in fact so different
that they started to wonder about each other.
John sent his disciples to Jesus
to ask him:
Are you really the one?
And Jesus answered:

You, John, are the greatest
of the OLD-TIMERS,
but the smallest of the NEW-TIMERS
is greater than you.
Something new had started,
the kingdom of God,
and we are invited into that
new kingdom,
the kingdom of the new era.
We are invited not only to profit passively,
but as well actively: to build it.
  Jesus compared the Jews with children.
  He said:
      You are like children;
      when John sang his funeral lament
      you did not weep;
      and now that I am singing,
      playing my melody
      on my flute,
      you are not dancing.
We should be dancing,
because of the promises made,
because of the kingdom of God.

3.

THE BAPTISM OF JESUS: GETTING INVOLVED

The baptism of Jesus
took place thirty years
after his birth.
It is, however,
celebrated in Christmas time,
immediately after his birth, his incarnation.
That is correct,
for his baptism too
belongs to the beginning,
the beginning of God's incarnation in this world.
    That incarnation
    is a wonderful event.
    It gives the final and ultimate assurance:
    God is with us.
    That incarnation was as well a slow process;
    it was not only a question of being born,
    but as well a question of the further steps
    to be taken,
    the further initiation rites.
First, he was presented for circumcision;
he got his name,
he was taken up;
then he went to the temple,
he got involved,
he asked questions,
he answered questions,
he got embedded,
he wanted to get involved.

14

Getting involved
is a painful process,
it is a hard way,
it is a continuous effort:
    A man knocks at your door,
    do not listen,
    you will get involved;
    a child takes her thumb out of her mouth,
    do not listen,
    you will get involved;
    your boss tells you about his temper,
    your son about his school,
    your daughter about her fears,
    your old mother about her loneliness,
    your friend about his frustrations,
    your cook about his family-problems,
    your aged father about his worries,
    your brother about his difficulties,
    your sister about her children,
    do not listen,
    you will get involved.
Every time that you listen,
it is going to cost you time,
and energy,
and involvement,
and very often money.
It eats you,
it needles you,
   and the clearer things get,
   and the clearer you let things get,
   the more time it is going to cost,
   the more energy,
   the more of your personality,
   and the more of your money.
It is at the moment
that Jesus left Nazareth
and stepped into the crowd
that he got involved.
   Up to that moment he had been hidden,

they had been ignorant of him,
and their ignorance meant his bliss.
Up to that moment he had been safe,
up to then he had been secure,
but at that moment that he stepped out into the open,
he got involved,
and his Father in heaven
in his excitement,
when he saw his Son stepping out,
could not keep his mouth shut,
and he shouted through all the heavens and the sky:
    This is my beloved son,
    there he is,
    watch him.
And Jesus revealed in that way,
"betrayed" in that way by his Father,
fled away
into the wilderness,
    to come out again,
    of course,
    to carry the burden
    of his involvement.
And he got tired,
very tired,
and in the end
he died on the cross.
    People did not leave him alone anymore.
    Modern authors
    have been very much under the impression
    of that aspect of Jesus' life.
Even D.H. Lawrence wrote
a rather heretical book
about it:
    how Jesus after his death-struggle on the cross
    woke up in his grave,
    and how he scrambled back to life
    and out of his grave,

how he found refuge in the house of an old lady,
and how he disappeared
again in life,
but now to live a different,
a totally uninvolved life.
His baptism,
his stepping into the crowd,
was a deliberate decision
to get involved,
to rub shoulders with all the others,
to be with the crowd,
to be with sinners,
to be with all.
   That is not our vocation,
   it is not your vocation,
   it is not my vocation,
   not with all and everybody.
   Impossible.
But it definitely is OUR vocation
to be involved,
with those
who may and should
claim us:
   your children,
   those entrusted to you,
   those dependent on you,
   your direct neighbors,
   the people you meet on your way.

4.

STEPPING IN THE MUD

Jesus stepped in the mud
of the river Jordan
in front of a large crowd
and his cousin John.
He wanted to be baptized,
he said.
John,
that cousin,
was horrified
when Jesus
bent before him
in the mud,
    and to understand the horror of John
    we must know something more about that mud.
Do you remember
the report of Noah, his ark, and his days?
In those days,
the Bible says,
people did not do anything but fashion wickedness,
all day long.
And do you remember
how in those days
people perished,
    with all their sins
    and all their works
    and all their children
    and all their ambitions
    in the mud,
    under the flood of water
    that lashed out over them

for forty days and forty nights
without any interruption.
When the ark rose out of the water,
it was surrounded by mud,
stifled with sin.
Do you remember
the report on Moses and his days?
How the Egyptians pestered his people
day and night,
how they made them work
without sufficient food,
frustrating them even in their family-life,
how they killed,
murdered,
arrested and detained,
and how all those Egyptians,
finally ended up
stuck in the mud
under the water of the Red Sea,
that gulfed
over them,
over their chariots,
over their horses,
their weapons,
and their evil intentions,
and how Moses and his people
rose out of that mud,
glorious and triumphant,
alleluia.
And when Moses and his people
looked back over the sea,
they saw the mud,
in which pharaoh
and all he stood for,
had perished:
a new order was born,
a new life started,
a new covenant was made.
But, again,

it did not last,
because John in his days
felt again the need,
a divinely inspired need,
to push the Jews of his time
in the mud of their own sinfulness,
and to wash them
into conversion,
to get them out of their sinfulness,
to get them out of their evil.
That evil is so evil.
Human evil is so irresponsible.
It is so stupid.
We know sufficient examples.
Our whole life is one example.
But let us take a glaring one.
In the year 1916,
on a line of about seventeen miles,
1,000,000 human beings killed each other
over a period of eight months,
that is at the average rate
of 4,000 men killed a day.
  The mud of human evil
  is very deep,
  it stinks forcefully,
  it is full of dangerous gases,
  and there was Jesus,
  in front of John,
  asking to be allowed
  to bend down in that mud.
  And John,
  no wonder,
  hesitated.
But he, Jesus,
he went down,
and when he came up,
the mud still streaming from his ears,
over his eyes

and his nose
into his mouth,
    HEAVEN OPENED,
    and a voice was heard,
    and a Spirit,
    a new Spirit in people,
    a new life
    and a new heart
    were announced,
    glory, glory, alleluia.
He was bathed in light,
he was drowned in God's voice,
he was full of spirit;
    but what about the mud,
    was he going to forget it?
    Was he going to overlook it
    in the new light?
    Was that Spirit going to cover up evil,
    was it going to work as a kind of consoling anesthetic,
    a kind of opium,
    bang,* ether,
    or chloroform?
It was not,
because once he got
the Spirit,
that Spirit drove him
into the desert,
and then again
out of the desert,
    to do his work
    in this world,
    to struggle with evil in us,
    in the world,
    in this world,
    in order to overcome it.

*Marijuana-like intoxicant

Part II

HIS PERSON

5.

ABBA AND AMEN

Nicodemus
came twice to Jesus.
Both times
he came during the night.
   He came to him for a night-discussion,
   and he came to him
   on the night of his death,
   when he helped to bury Jesus.
He must have been waiting
for a very dark,
moonless night
that first time,
because he did not want
to be seen:
   People were asleep,
   the watchmen had settled down
   in their corners,
   all dogs were asleep
   in their small circle;
   steps were heard,
   but nobody was seen,
   and small children
   were smacking their lips
   in their sleep,
   as if they were tasting better things
   than this world,
   but then turning around
   slept on
   on their other side.

He came during the night.
During the night
we do not see.
Everything is there all right:
   the trees,
   the animals,
   the stones,
   the roads,
   and the people.
But we do not see.
Nicodemus came not to ask
about those trees, animals, stones, roads, and people.
He came to ask
about the things
hiding behind them,
hiding behind all this.
Nicodemus was a religious man.
   Nicodemus knew a lot,
   he was a scribe,
   he knew all the stories of his people,
   he knew their meaning,
   he knew Genesis,
   and the book of Kings,
   the law,
   and the prophets,
   he knew sufficiently
   to be able to say to Jesus:
   I know that you were sent
   from God.
He said:
I know,
   and yet
   he was wondering about it all.
Humankind has known so much
all the time,
in all kinds of traditions.
People have always known
that behind all this

and that,
behind him
and her,
behind the earth
and the sky,
behind birth
and death,
there is hiding
in the dark
something,
somebody.
And Nicodemus
came to ask
out of his darkness,
out of the darkness left,
whether Jesus knew
what it was all about.
Just like others came to him
and are coming to him,
from within their own
African or other traditions
to ask to clear
the questions
that seemed to have
remained unsolved.
And Jesus speaks
and speaks:
about coming out of the dark,
about coming into the light,
about saving
and eternal life,
about a sentence pronounced,
about a Father and a Son,
about a Spirit,
and actions that are going to be
exposed.
But even then,
after all this,

things remain vague.
   What did he want?
   What did he propose?
   What did he mean?
   Was he not dodging the issue?
   Did he, maybe, not trust Nicodemus?
   Was he afraid to be with an
   informer?
There are scholars
who have been studying the texts
of the New Testament,
who have been comparing texts
for ages,
to find out
which words
were definitely spoken by Jesus,
his authentic words
his authentic answers,
his verba ipisissima,
and some of them hold
that we can be certain
of only two words:
   AMEN
   and
   ABBA.
At first hearing
this sounds odd,
if not ridiculous
and unbelievable:
a mountain bringing forth
a mouse:
   AMEN,
   meaning something like:
   "Let it be"
   or
   "It is God who speaks."
   ABBA
   meaning:
   pappa

baba
daddy
papa
father.
And yet these two words
sum up
all that Jesus wanted to say.
He,
Jesus,
said:
    It is God who speaks,
    he wants to be called
    by you
    ABBA
    he wants to be
    our father.
And all the rest
flows forth from that
as the consequences
in the life of Christ:
    his prayer,
    his attitude,
    his goodness,
    his anger,
    his healing,
    his cursing,
    his blessing,
    his day-life,
    his night-life,
    his sharing,
    his refusing:
        ABBA
        AMEN,
        and our life
        is a christlike life
        and as far as we too
        realize that
        ABBA
        AMEN.

6.

HE AND HIS
KIND OF KINGDOM

We are celebrating the solemnity,
as it is very royally called,
of the universal kingship of Jesus Christ.
King, world, church, oikoumene,
they all seem to hang together,
    and yet that whole kingship of Christ
    is a rather confusing issue;
    it is even, I think,
    a rather fishy issue.
    Did that man,
    Jesus,
    want to be a king?
When the devil wanted to make him a king,
he refused;
when the people wanted to make him a king,
he ran away into the forest;
when Pilate asked him:
    Now tell me,
    Are you a king?
He answered:
    That is what you say,
    but not from here,
    not from this world, not like you;
    my power is different;
    if it would not be different,
    then you would have been crushed by now
    by my father's angels
    and their missiles.

His power was not from here.
We all know where the power from here comes from:
    It comes from what somebody HAS;
    at the roadblocks in the streets of Kenya,
    the matatu,* the ex-hare-krishna car,
    is stopped time and time again,
    trunks are opened,
    briefcases are investigated,
    pockets are turned out,
    and the shiny Mercedes Benz 280 SE,
    according to the Automobile Association,
    the most expensive car for sale in the Republic,
    costing 249,918 Kenya shillings,
    is not even stopped.
The man in the matatu
is asked to justify
    the 60 shillings in his pocket,
    the guitar over his shoulders,
    the bag next to him,
    but nobody ever asks the owner of the Benz
    where he got his 249,918 shillings from.
His power was not from here.
We all know where the power from here comes from:
    It comes from your place on the social ladder,
    it comes from your place in society,
    it comes from your function and role.
    You are waiting in a long queue,
    a wananchi queue,†
    the waiting is long, boring, and painful,
    and there a man passes in front of you,
    a man who says:
        I am the permanent secretary,
        I am the dean,
        I am the director,

*The cheapest possible "taxis," these cars are sometimes twenty or more years old.

†A queue of the common people.

I am a professor,
I am a student leader.
And they,
they are helped first,
they are helped best,
they get the single room.
His power was not from here.
We all know where the power from here comes from:
It comes from what you can do;
everybody is continually asking:
Who can do something about this,
who is the boss over here,
whose signature do I need,
and if you cannot do anything about it,
if your signature does not mean a thing,
and if you are powerless,
you are null and void,
your name means nothing,
you are negligible.
Jesus' power was not from this world;
this world is no good,
this world is a shame,
this world is corrupt,
this world is split by people.
In this world people are not respected
because they are people;
they are respected
because they are rich,
because they are white, or
because they are black.
In this world people are not respected
because they are people;
they are respected
because of their function,
because they wear a uniform,
because they wear a badge or seven stripes,
because they have a miter or a mortar board
on top of their head.

In this world people are not respected
because they are people;
they are respected
   because they are influential
   because they are important.
The have-nots,
who respects the have-nots?
The people without function,
who respects the unemployed?
They are picked up as vagrants,
and that is what they are according to the law.
The people who are not important,
who respects the people who are not important?
Who speaks to them,
who cares for them?
And that is why so many children
run around half-dressed
and half-fed.
All that is this world.
This world lacks interest in people,
in its people.
   And he said:
   Nobody among you
   should be called master,
   or teacher,
   or father.
   And when they asked him
   who is the most important,
   he took a small smelly unwashed streetboy
   and said: This one.
This Jesus,
this universal king,
showed us
that our whole attitude should change,
that our world should change
in a revolutionary way,
   that we should respect all people
   for the simple and only fact

that they happen to be God's people;
that we should respect all people
because they are his sheep,
the lean ones and the fat ones;
that we should respect all people,
because he knows their names,
    he knows the name of that small girl,
    that virgin,
    that spring-chicken
    (what a lack of respect to call her that name)
    who is bribed to spread her legs
    because of the power of that rich man from town.
    He knows the name of that prostitute
    who was arrested in the street
    because an international church meeting
    was going on in town;
    and he respects her
    as much
    as he respects the archbishop of Canterbury,
    or Cardinal Otunga,
    or any of our guests;
    he knows the name of the beggar in the street;
    he knows the name of the man
    at the end of the queue;
    he knows the names of the destitute children
    all over the world;
    he knows all their names;
    after all he made them,
    and he made them all alike,
and there he is standing as a shepherd,
in the middle of his scattered sheep,
keeping them in view,
rescuing them from mist and darkness,
looking for the lost ones,
trying to bring back the stray ones,
bandaging the wounded ones,
making the weak ones strong,
looking after the tall and the small,
the rich and the poor.

That is his power,
that is his kingdom,
knowing their names.
He is not interested
   in their cars,
   in the quality of their clothes,
   in their degrees,
   in their prizes and awards,
   in their grades and decorations,
   in their functions and ordinations,
   in their success and their training;
he knows their names,
he knows *them,*
and he wishes them all well,
   and all they need.
And that is how we should behave,
and that is why the world should change,
in the east,
in the west,
in the north,
and in the south.
That is how he frees us
from deception and fake glory.
That is how he liberates us
from shortsightedness
and injustice.
That is how he enables us
to see the world as it should be,
an oikoumene,
a humanly inhabited world,
where there is place and time
for everybody.
A world in which people will not only be with each other,
but a world in which people will be for each other.
   It seems a dream.
   It is a dream,
   in *this* world.
   But neither this world
   nor its leaders

will have the last word.
If this world
and its leaders
would have the last word,
then there is no hope.
HE will have the last word.
HE is the king,
 and that is why there is hope,
 for everybody,
 for you
 and for me,
 and that is final liberation.

7.

JESUS DID NOT MARRY

An angel fell down from heaven,
it entered a small room in Nazareth,
and God made his home in this world.
Up to then
God had been the maker of this world,
its conceiver,
its upholder,
its caretaker,
its sacred center.
   Now,
   over there in Nazareth,
   he decided
   to pitch his tent with us,
   really with us
   and not only in a cloud in a temple
   or in a tabernacle.
He decided to have
his roof
between our roofs,
to have his fireplace
in the midst of our fireplaces,
to have his cooking pot
together with our cooking pots,
   and he did this
   by looking for a human partner.
   Just like anybody
   who likes to start a home
   in this world
   looks for a partner.

You cannot start a home alone.
If you visit the house of a man alone,
you can see immediately
that somebody is missing,
something is lacking
because somebody is lacking.
And when you go to the house of a woman alone,
there is
in another way
that very same impression.
    Man needs a partner
    to start and keep a home.
    Woman needs a partner
    to start and keep a home.
    God needed a partner,
    to find a roof,
    and a fire,
    water and food,
    milk and care,
    security and a baby-cot,
    education and a family
    for his SON in this world.
    He chose Mary.
And when that virgin Mary
said: YES,
all he needed was provided:
    the womb,
    the body,
    the milk,
    the water,
    the diapers,
    the bread,
    the salt,
    the roof,
    the baby-cot
    and the care.
It is then
that his Son

could really become EMMANUEL,
that is, God with us.
    That son of his and hers
    grew up.
    He left his home.
    He went into the desert,
    he came out of the desert,
    he was baptized by John the Baptist,
    he started to travel around.
    But that son of his and hers
    never settled down.
Did you ever hear of the town
in which Jesus had his own house?
Did you ever hear of the name
of such a building,
or about the number of his flat?
He did not settle,
he did not even choose a partner.
He never started his own home;
he had friends,
plenty of them,
he had his lady-friends,
plenty of them,
but every time
they wanted to keep him,
to make him settle,
or to lay a special claim on him,
he would say things like:
    Do not keep me,
    I have to go on,
    others are waiting,
    do not hold me,
    let me go.
And he went apparently
forgetting
    about his mother,
    about his family,
    about his parental home,

    about Nazareth,
    about Judea,
    about Galilee,
    about his country,
    and about his nation.
His disciples did not understand this,
although he asked some of them
to do the same:
    to leave their father,
    to leave their mother,
    to leave their brothers and sisters,
    their wives,
    and consequently their homes.
The disciples did not understand
that he could not choose,
that he would not choose,
that he could not make up his mind
about one partner,
with that color of eyes,
with that height,
with a birth-mark here or there,
and that identity-card number.
    They did not understand
    that he as the Son of God
    could not settle down
    with a wife
    and some children,
    with four or six or eight chairs
    and a table
    with a coffee pot
    and a dog,
    in a house
    on such-and-such street
    at number 40
    in that flat D-32
    with that green paint on the front door.
He could not do that,
he would not do that,

because he wanted to be at home
with the whole of humankind,
with everybody.
    He did not forbid people to marry,
    he did not forbid us to start our own homes.
    He was at CANA,
    and to approve
    of what was happening over there
    he gave at that wedding
    the possibility
    to all
    to have a good drink,
    maybe even too good a drink for some.
He told people
to be faithful in their marriage,
not to run away from each other.
He hated people
who did not take care
of their children,
    but he added to all that
    a new dimension,
    that general brotherhood idea,
    that family of God idea,
    that world perspective.
He added
the necessity of looking further
than our own family alone;
he added that idea
of taking care of
all our neighbors,
and he wanted to make us wish,
and wish it effectively,
what he himself wished,
and he wished it very effectively:
    PEACE AND GOODNESS
    TO ALL PEOPLE.

8.

WAS HE POOR?

They say
that Jesus was poor.
They say
that they say
that Jesus was poor
to keep us poor.
It is a plot,
a plot from the west,
to keep us low.
   But was he poor?
   He, who blew or spat at a piece of bread,
   and it started to grow,
   and to grow,
   and to grow,
   so that it could feed 3,000,
     and again 3,000.
   Was he poor?
   The couple of Cana was poor,
   because they had not sufficient wine,
   or what we would call beer,*
   to keep their guests going,
   but he,
   was he poor?
   He told them to fill up
     all casks,
     all pots,
     all pans,

*Beer is the preferred beverage at major celebrations in East Africa.

    all containers,
    all jugs,
    with water,
    pure, plain water,
and then he pointed at that water,
all that water,
or he blew over it,
or he spat at it,
or he simply touched it,
and all that water changed,
blushing when seeing its master,
and it became wine,
first-class wine,
A-level grade,
bucketsfull,
wine for everybody.
Was he poor?
He, who when asked to pay his taxes
pointed at a fish
swimming in the water
in a nearby pond.
They caught the fish;
he opened its mouth,
and he produced
from that mouth
all the money they wanted.
Was he poor,
he who had a purse
in which was so much money
that Judas could take the risk
to steal from it
without being noticed?
Was he poor,
he who was wearing such a first-class shirt
at the moment of his death,
without so much as a seam,
that they decided
not to tear it up,
because it was so nice?

But, was he not born in a stable?
Oh, yes, he was,
but if your family cannot pay for a hotel
on the weekend
when all the citizens have to register,
and every place is overcrowded,
then that does not necessarily mean
that you are without means.
But he had no stone to lay his head on
during the night!
Do you believe that?
Do you really believe
that when he,
   the miracle worker,
who brought life,
pure human life,
wherever he came,
   that he with those miracle-hands
   would not find a bed to sleep in?
Do you really mean to say
that you think
that the doors remained closed to him?
His difficulty must have been
to make a choice
in what bed to sleep.
   No, he was not poor,
   at least not in that way.
   He had plenty of fish,
   he had plenty of wine,
   he had plenty of bread,
   he had plenty of friends,
   he was not undernourished,
   he was not underfed,
   he was not naked,
   he was not without a shelter,
      because that is what poverty means:
      to be underfed,
      to be undernourished,

to be without a shelter,
to be without security,
not certain about how to eat,
   how to drink,
   how to survive,
   for the next twelve hours.
He was not like that.
All that has to be fought against
by the whole of humankind.
He was not like that.
They called him "poor"
for another reason,
for the reason that combats
the poverty we spoke about.
For a reason that asks much of us,
for a reason that challenges us.
 Paul gave that reason,
 when he wrote
 that that man Jesus,
 the Son of God,
 the maker of all that is
 and of all that will be,
 did not keep
 all he had
 and all he is
 for himself alone,
 but that he came down
 on this earth
 to share with us
 his life
 and his power.
And that is why
that wherever he went,
power went out of him,
 out of his hands,
  that healed;
 out of his breath,
  that healed;

out of his spittle,
　　that healed;
out of his eyes,
　　that healed;
out of his dress,
　　that healed.
Wherever he came,
he was the center of sharing
and giving,
and making his own power
overflow to others.
　　And he died on the cross
　　with his arms wide open,
　　naked,
　　not able to hide anything,
　　openly giving everything
　　even for those
　　who under the cross
　　shouted at him:
　　　　save yourself,
　　　　and we will believe,
　　　　think of yourself,
　　　　and we will follow you.
　　He did not listen,
　　but gave and gave
　　himself for all,
　　introducing
　　a style of life
　　that only can save the world,
　　and that will overcome
　　the poverty
　　and the misery,
　　the hunger
　　and the thirst,
　　the pains
　　and the sorrows
　　of all.

9.

HE ALWAYS SAID
YES AND AMEN

Everybody knows
what dialectics is about.
Everybody knows
even if we do not know
exactly
about the complicated ways
in which philosophers
from all ages
and from all over our planet
have been explaining its laws.
Everybody knows,
because everybody is aware
of the tempting and unavoidable
laws
of human speech.
   If you say very clearly
   and outspokenly: YES,
   then you can be pretty sure
   that somebody else
   is going to say as clearly
   and as outspokenly: No.
   And the more outspoken your YES
   the more outspoken their No.
That is how human conversations,
how human relations,
and how human discussions
work
or do not work.

Jesus participated
in this type of dialectics,
in this game
people play with each other,
just like he participated
in all things human.
When Jesus said: YES,
Peter,
Philip,
or someone else
would say:
No.
But there was a difference,
Jesus was rarely found to be
on the No side of things.
He was more often than not
on the YES side.
   One evening Peter lands his boat.
   Jesus is on the shore
   waiting for some fish.
   Peter had caught nothing.
   He said:
     Too bad,
     no fish tonight.
   But Jesus said:
       Oh, yes,
       there is fish,
       plenty of fish,
       throw out your net,
       I am sure.
   And Peter with a sigh,
   and a wink of his eye
   to his comrades,
   because of this obviously
   stupid suggestion
   of that non-fisherman,
   that son of a carpenter,
   that utter layman,

that desert-rat,
throws out his net.
And he got that net,
and later his big mouth
full of fish,
freshly caught fish.
His mother came to him
at Cana.
She said:
  Too bad,
  no wine any more.
He said:
  No wine?
  Oh, yes, there is.
And he went to the kitchen
to have a look,
and he changed all the available water
into wine,
into A-grade wine,
and he took care
that his mother
got one
of the first cups.
   They were standing in a crowd,
   it was getting late,
   and Philip said
   (I think it was Philip,
   I am not sure,
   I did not look it up)
   Philip said:
    Too bad,
    there is no food.
He said:
  No food?
  Oh, yes, there is.
And he asked:
  Is there anybody
  with some food?

And a small boy
who had been standing there
all the time,
with his mouth wide open
looking at Jesus
felt under his shirt,
and shouted:
    Yes, Sir,
     over here.
And when everybody looked
and laughed
when they saw his piece of fish
and his pieces of bread,
he blushed
and felt ashamed.
But Jesus said:
    So there is food,
    I told you so.
And he broke it,
he broke it,
he broke it
thousands of times
the food of that small boy.
  Jairus came up to him
  and said:
    My daughter is dead,
    there is no life in her any more,
    useless,
    finished.
And he said:
    Do not say that,
    oh, yes, there is,
    she has some life,
    she is asleep.
And he went with the weeping crowd
to show his yes.
And he did prove it,
because only some minutes later

    that daughter was being seen
    sitting at a kitchen table
    with a cup of milk
    and munching a piece of
    warmed up mutton.
Jesus is the YES and AMEN,
and AMEN means YES.
He is the YES and AMEN sayer.
    When all say:
        There is nothing,
        no life,
        no food,
        no drink,
        no sight,
        no hearing,
        no muscles,
        no brains,
        no growth,
        no hope.
    He says:
        Oh, yes,
        there is life,
        there is food,
        there is drink,
        there is sight,
        there is hearing,
        there are muscles,
        there are brains,
        there is growth,
        there is hope.
He, himself,
gave all kinds of stories
to prove
and to illustrate this point:
    about a pearl hidden in the field,
    about life hidden in seed,
    about light put under a bucket,
    about some money hidden in a room.

He reveals the positive side
of reality
in his type of dialectics.
   He is, after all, the maker,
   he knows what it is all about,
   he knows the big print,
   but he knows as well
   what is hidden in the small print
   of the world,
   of each of us.
And the most grandiose step
in this type of dialectical development
came
when those disciples of his,
sitting hidden in an upper room
without any confidence in themselves,
afraid,
scared,
nervous,
itchy,
and good for nothing,
   suddenly felt uplifted
   in themselves,
   when it suddenly dawned upon them
   that is was not No
   but Yes,
   that they had possibilities,
   they had never dreamt of,
   and real content
   and real life
   and real Spirit.
The life of the Spirit in them,
they thought No,
it is all finished,
it is all over.
   He said Yes,
   it still has to begin,
   and they remained faithful,

they lived in common,
they broke their bread,
they prayed
and went out,
and through them
he came to you
and to me.

10.

HE AND DEVELOPMENT

Everybody seems to know
what development is about.
That does not mean
that they all agree.
Some restrict it to something
in the economical field.
Development according to them means:
    more wealth,
    more material welfare,
    more money,
    more industries,
    more coffee,
    more tea,
    fatter cows,
    disease free corn,
    and more sisal.
Others include
other
more human values
when they speak
about that same development:
    more schools,
    less ignorance;
    more clinics,
    less sickness;
    more human dignity,
    less dependency;
    better housing,
    less despondency.

All these items
are obviously and doubtlessly
very good.
Followers of Jesus Christ
should agree full-heartedly
with the promotion
of all those things.
 Is it not true
 that Jesus fed the hungry,
 that he made wine for the thirsty,
 that he healed the sick,
 that he gave hearing to the deaf,
 and sight to the blind,
 that he informed the ignorant?
But he did not do
only that.
He added another dimension.
He intended as well
growth in another field.
He saw through all this
a SPIRIT divine,
a Spirit trying to bring
people together.
 He saw a plan,
 a divine plan,
 of growth and development.
 He dreamt about a community of all people.
 He did not only dream about it,
 he spoke about it.
 He did not only speak about it,
 he worked and died for it.
 He called it his kingdom.
 He was so serious about that community,
 that he even called it HIS BODY,
and he gave his life,
and his blood,
his talents,
his head,

and his heart
for that BODY.
   He used parables
   and symbols
   to illustrate
   what he meant:
      a tree full of birds,
      a shed full of sheep,
      a plant full with leaves,
      a net filled with fish,
      a table surrounded by guests,
      the NEW TEMPLE OF GOD.
We as his followers
can only be his followers
along those lines,
under those conditions.
We as his followers
can only be his followers
insofar as we direct
our activities and passivities
accordingly.
   We should be the champions
   of that BODY,
   in an effort
   of integral
   human
   development.

11.

HIS AUTHORITY

One of the things
people around Jesus
mentioned about him,
even several times,
is the fact that he spoke,
and was,
with authority.
   What is authority?
   You might have seen on the campus
   over the last week
   a rather strange looking man,
   with a bunch of flowers around his neck,
   and an arrow of gold painted down his nose,
   with a little tail on top of his head,
   and a bag over his shoulder,
   a bag filled with holy texts.
He was a member
of the Hare Krishna movement.
He came to my office
to ask
where he would be able to meet students,
and while he was explaining his point of view,
he said during our conversation
several times:
   my spiritual master used to say,
   my guru told me,
   my spiritual guide advised me,
   and things like that.

He referred several times
to somebody else,
whom he took very seriously,
because,
obviously,
that person was considered by him
as an authority.
    There are very many people
    who say
    that they are against authority.
    They are not going to go to anybody
    "in authority,"
    even when they would be in difficulties.
    They are not going to go to a professor,
    they are not going to go to a warden,
    they are not going to go to the dean,
    they are not going to go to a priest,
    they are not going to go to the doctor,
    they are not going to go to an older person,
    because they do not believe
    in the authority of those people,
    or they do not accept their authority,
    if only because all those people
    are over thirty.
    And who trusts anybody over thirty,
    except those who are over thirty
    themselves already?
And after having said all this,
they sit down
together with others,
together with those of their own age,
and speaking together,
they sometimes even formulate
their anti-authoritarian points of view
on the authority
of their age group.
What does authority mean?
I think

that we might say
that it means
the acceptance
in our life
of an influence
or a force
that makes us grow.
The Latin root
of the word authority
can be translated
as
    growthmaker,
    enlarger,
    or something like that.
That Hare Krishna man
definitely experienced
in his life
that spiritual leader of his
as an influence
that made him see,
that made him hear,
that made him feel,
that made him grow.
    I think that that is
    exactly
    what the people around Jesus
    felt about him.
    He and his words did not leave you
    untouched.
    He made you feel what
    human life was about,
    what God is about,
    and things like that.
    He had AUTHORITY
    and his disciples were willing
    to listen
    because he made you
    grow.

Real authority
has everything
to do with growth.
It is not something wild,
it is not shouting
at the top of your voice:
I am the boss,
and *you* have to obey,
I am going to force you,
I am going to kick you,
I even can fire you,
or something like that.
>All that is not authority,
>that is power.
>And power is not authority,
>if only because of Christ's
>powerlessness.

Anybody
who is in authority
should take that into
consideration.
A father
who has authority over his son
should make his son grow
under the influence of his
authority.
>Those who hold authority in the church
>have that authority
>when they are helping others
>to grow in Christ,
>and that means to grow
>>in justice
>>and peace
>>in love
>>and in truth.
>And those in political power
>have only authority
>insofar as they help

the population
to develop and to grow.
In other words,
authority
is an influence,
and it should always be
a healthy influence.
It is a builder,
a constructive element.
It is a precious gift,
and we all should pray
to meet somebody
with that type of authority
in our life.
Because they will be
our best friends
and we all need them
badly,
because we all should grow.

12.

HE IS SPLENDID,
ARE WE STUPID?

We had this week
over here in Nairobi,
a seminar:
CHRISTIANITY IN INDEPENDENT AFRICA.
The opinions expressed
varied from belief in Jesus,
to saying
that that man Jesus from Nazareth
had no message whatsoever,
or hardly any message,
to the nations of Africa.
   Yet, God's prophets
   called him the light of the nations;
   and he knew himself
   to be the light and the truth.
If he is the light,
if he is the truth,
if he is splendid,
   does that mean
   that we,
   Africans or not,
   are dark,
   dull, unreflective,
   and stupid?
To come to the point,
let us consider some human experiences,

the human experience of that boy and that girl.
She was eighteen.
He was eighteen.
    She was wondering
    whether she was all right
    when she looked at herself
    in the piece of mirror she had.
    Was she all right?
    She had her doubts.
    She was very unsure.
    Was she well proportioned?
    She tried to look at her breasts,
    were they too small,
    were they too tall,
    she could not tell,
    because she could not see.
    She thought she might be able to see
    while looking at her reflection in the water.
    So she went to a pond,
    but standing in front of that pond,
    she realized that she saw herself
    at such an awkward angle
    that she could not see anything at all
    without falling into the water.
    And even then,
    what about her reverse parts,
    too high,
    too low,
    too fat,
    too skinny,
    how would she be able to tell?
    And that was not all,
    and she wrote a letter to the problem post
    of the *Daily Nation**
    to Susannah Scott:

*Nairobi daily newspaper

Dear Susan,
I am so unsure of myself. I am so silly, while all the others
are talking, I never have anything to say. I am so afraid
that my legs are too short and my mouth too big, what
should I do? Answer me quickly. Please.
He was eighteen too,
very broad in his shoulders,
very narrow in his hips.
He was pretty sure
to be completely out of proportion,
because when he popped in at the pop-in
self-selection stores
he needed for his chest
the EXTRA LARGE size
and for his hips
SMALL.
And another real problem
that worried him
was,
that he was never sure
what to say.
Everybody around him
was wiser
and deeper
and obviously better informed,
so he preferred
to keep his mouth
shut.
He had no contribution
to make.
   AND THEN
   THEY MET
      when he saw her,
      and when she saw him,
      he said:
         My god,
      and she turned away;

in fact she did it in such a way
that she could have
a better look at him.
He said:
   You are so beautiful.
She said:
   You have words of wisdom.
He said:
   You are so witty.
She said:
   You look so strong.
And he had no doubts about himself any more,
and she became the most self-reliant mother
you ever saw.
That is what people,
what friends do to each other.
It is in this way
that we discover ourselves.
It is in this way that Jesus
wants to be a light.
   A light does not add
   so very much;
   it adds visibility.
   We can see
   in the light
   what we did not see
   before.
Light does not only enable us to see,
it enables us to do things
we never thought of
before.
   Jesus makes us see
   who we are,
   how we are,
   what we can do.
   All things we would not have been able
   to discover

so easily
by and on our own
in ourselves,
or
in our restricted circle.
He took care that someone
whispered in the ear of his mother:
You are full of grace.
He told Peter:
You are the rock.
He told Nathanael:
You are just.
He told Zaccheus:
You are good.
He told Judas:
You are my friend.
He told his murderers:
You do not know what you are doing.
He told us,
each of us:
You are a child of God.
   It is in this
   his light
   that we,
   Africans or not,
   discover ourselves,
   that we discover our possibilities
   as well as our tasks.
It is in this
his light,
that we discover
in our own traditional cultures
ourselves,
our possibilities,
and our tasks.
   He is splendid,
   but that does not mean
   that we are stupid.

13.

THAT IS HUMILITY FOR YOU

There is the story
about two guests invited to a meal,
and both of them
took the wrong place.
   One had to go down
   and that was a shame;
   one had to go up
   and that was a rather dubious honor,
   because even he seemed
   to have made a mistake.
Both made a mistake.
Both were corrected.
The story is very often said
to be about humility.
One of the most ancient experts
in that matter
was Saint Benedict.
He spoke about a ladder
leading up to real humility.
That ladder had according to him
twelve steps.
It is no use to give you
the whole of that ingenious structure.
   It suffices for our purpose
   to know
   that at the sixth step
   the humble man considers himself
   as a useless servant

67

(not too helpful an attitude)
worthy of the lowest and the meanest
(not very much of a personality booster either);
at the twelfth step
the humble man is so far
that he does not look up anymore,
he is constantly reminding himself
of his unworthiness in God's eyes,
and whether he is in a liturgical ceremony,
in the garden,
or in the street,
his head is bent,
and he continuously
tries to look
at an imaginery spot
three feet in front of him
on the soil
he happens to walk on.
    No boasting,
    not even about his humility,
    no raising of his voice,
    nothing.
    Although there might have been
    in his heart
    that remaining hope,
    that someone,
    preferably,
    but not necessarily, God
    would say:
    Move higher up.
All this is nice,
but it does not correspond
to what Jesus wanted to explain.
He, of course, once said:
    Come to me, because
    I am humble of heart.
    And that does not seem to be
    too humble a statement.

He even added things like:
Nobody knows the Father
except me.
Nobody can come to the Father
except through me.
That Jesus
seems to be terribly conscious
and very well aware indeed,
of his value.
He does not seem
to have been humble
in a Benedictine way.
He elevated himself in a way
nobody ever did,
before or after.
He got the greatest possible publicity in the world.
And even two thousand years after his death
his greatest publicity stunt,
his resurrection,
still attracts attention
from all over the world.
So much so that people even tried to imitate him.
    Did you not read
    some days ago
    about that man in the Kenyan town of Meru,
    who said
    that he could hang himself,
    die,
    and rise from death?
    There were very many spectators,
    there was a whole school to look:
    He bound a rope to a branch,
    he put the noose around his neck,
    he let go,
    and he did die,
    never to come out of death again.
Jesus was convinced of his uniqueness,
and he was right,

he was unique,
and there was no lack of humility
in admitting his rightful place
in this world.
    And yet he considered himself
    as part of a whole,
    and that is humility
    for you.
You are unique,
I am unique too.
Do you not think
that I am unique?
I think so,
but you too.
    God never imitates himself,
    poor authors do,
    they write one book,
    one bestseller,
    and then another one
    in which they only repeat
    themselves.
God never repeats himself.
Think of the number of noses in the world,
all different;
think of the number of ears,
all different,
some are even more different
than others.
    God does not lack inspiration,
    he goes on being creative.
    You are unique,
    no doubt about that,
    and we might thank heavens
    because of it,
    because too many of you,
    or too many of me,
    would be disastrous.

You are unique,
but you are not alone,
we are all parts of a very large whole.
We are members of a terrifically
complicated human society.
Each one has to play their part,
we belong together
like the players in a band:
    the drums,
    the trumpet,
    the saxophone,
    the two electrical guitars,
    and the organ,
    each playing their instrument,
    each playing their part.
To know
that one is unique,
and yet part,
part of a big band,
that is humility.
    Humility is rightly called a virtue,
    it is a sentiment,
    it is knowing your place
    in the fullest sense of the word
    within this world
    within this society.

Part III

WORDS, DEEDS, DISCIPLES

14.

WORDS HAVE POWER

Words have power,
human words have a tremendous power:
    Do you forgive me?
    Please say something,
    Do you forgive me?
    Yes, I forgive you.
    I love you.
    I love you so much,
    do you love me?
    Please say something,
    Do you love me?
    Yes, I do.
    Otieno, do you want to take Atieno as your lawful wife?
    Yes, I do.
    Atieno, do you want Otieno as your lawful husband?
    No, I don't.
Words have power,
human words have a tremendous power:
    They can heal, unite, divide, disrupt;
    they can ask, forgive, answer, command;
    they can coax, tempt, frighten, soothe;
    they can make you sleepy and wide awake;
    they can kill and give life;
    they can lie;
    they can tell the truth;
    they can say nothing;
    they can say everything.
And in the Bible,
and Bible really means "words,"
it is the same:

God said:
   Sky,
   and there was sky;
   water,
   and there was water;
   land,
   and there was land;
   woman,
   and there stood Eve.
God said: Adam,
  and he went hiding behind a bush;
God said: Cain,
  and he looked up;
God said: Moses,
  lead my people;
God said: Jeremiah,
  you are my prophet;
God said: Isaiah,
  listen, for it is Yahweh who speaks;
God said: Mary,
  and she said: Here I am.
Words make people look up,
  and look back;
  they make them hasten
  and slow down;
  they make them turn to the right,
  and to the left,
  stop and go on.
  God's words are full of power;
  they filled the womb of the Blessed Virgin,
  and Mary blushed
  and fell in love.
  Jesus' words have power;
  he said:
    Girl, I tell you come back to life,
    and she did
    and started to jump and dance.
But our words too have power,

tremendous power,
power over God,
for he said also:
    Ask,
    and I am going to hear you;
    open your mouth,
    and I will be there.
He, God, said:
    I heard you shouting
    and I could not forget.
Jesus listened to everybody
who shouted at him,
even if it was
from the gutter of the street.
We can call upon God with words,
we can say: My God, my God.
He will listen;
we may shout:
    Father, help,
    Father, forgive,
    Father, heal;
    he will help,
    he will forgive,
    he will heal.
That is why our words
play such an important role during our liturgy:
    We pray,
    we sing,
    we acclaim,
    or better:
    we should pray,
    we should sing,
    we should acclaim,
    we should participate.
We are often too dull,
    too listless,
    too much mumbling;
    we should participate.

Human words are so powerful,
that some words
are even capable
of changing the bread and the wine,
our food
and our drink,
into Jesus Christ himself,
because he once took bread and said: Change,
because he once took the wine and said: Change,
because he gave the bread and the wine to his disciples
and said: Change.
    Form the new community,
    form the new people,
    the people of God.
    Words are very important.
    Words can put the world in order
    and disorder.
Only the words of Jesus
can put the world straight.
Let us listen to those words,
let us speak out those words aloud,
let us use his words:
    He preached,
    he blessed,
    he cursed,
    he shouted,
    he whispered,
    he cried,
    he stammered,
    to bring harmony,
    justice, and peace.
    He was even called the word,
    the word that is going to change the world,
    just like our words,
    his words we speak
    will change
    this whole wide world.

15.

THE SERMON
ON THE MOUNTAIN

It all started on a mountain,
in fact it was not so very much of a mountain,
only a bump on the landscape.
But he was standing on top of it,
and that day it became a real mountain,
a mountain of men and women
coming from all sides.
It was like the slope above Uhuru Park
in front of the East African Community building.
On a normal day that slope is insignificant,
just grass and some rocks,
but when it fills with people
on a national feastday,
on Kenyatta day or so,
then it becomes enormous,
a mountain of people.
　　They came in hundreds,
　　they came in thousands,
　　and Jesus was in the middle.
　　Why did they come?
　　Did they come to hear
　　his sermon on the mountain?
　　Did they come expecting to hear
　　about the beatitudes?
　　I really doubt it.
　　They were curious
　　AND they wanted to touch him.

79

If you would have asked
  the Levis,
  the Marias,
  the Josephs,
  the Magdalenas,
  and the Simeons,
  why they came,
  they most probably would have answered,
  looking around whether others
  were not listening in:
  I got a sore tooth,
  I got piles,
  I have a persistent skin-disease,
  I cannot get rid of my constipation,
  my foot has been hurting me
  over the last two months.
They wanted to be healed,
they wanted to be happy.
Then he started to speak.
He was not going to heal
that day,
he was not going to work miracles
that day.
He was going to try something else.
He was going to try to change
their destiny,
their outlook on life.
And he said:
  Blessed are the poor in spirit,
  for theirs is the kingdom of heaven,
  and
  woe to the rich,
  for they got their consolation already,
  before their time.
He began with the poor.
He did not call the poor happy.
Poverty is not happiness.
Poverty is injustice done somewhere.

He spoke about the poor of spirit
   and the poor of spirit
   are those who do not contain themselves,
   who did not define themselves,
   who did not close themselves,
   the poor of spirit
   are those
   who are still open,
   who do not believe
   that they have arrived as yet.
A man who is completely taken up
by what he has,
that man is not poor in spirit;
a student who has planned
his whole career,
that student is not poor in spirit;
a scholar who thinks
that he knows everything already,
that scholar is not poor in spirit.
   Those people are possessors,
   and they are possessed,
   they are rich,
   and they are unhappy
   maybe without realizing it.
   Christ said that they got their consolation already,
   but someone speaks about consolation,
   only when one is sad and frustrated.
Happy are the poor in spirit
means
happy are those people
who did not settle down,
who did not pin themselves down,
who did not yet organize themselves definitely,
because up to now
they did not yet know sufficiently
about themselves,
about others,
and about the world.

Happy are those people
who do not accept things as they are,
who do not possess
and who are not possessed.
Happy are those people
who are still open,
because theirs is the kingdom of heaven,
for them the heavenly sky is the limit.
They are the ones
who have their doubts
about this kingdom of earth;
they are the ones
who know
that there is not too much justice as yet.
They are the ones
who know
that notwithstanding
all official and unofficial propaganda
a lot has still to be done.
    The poor in spirit are the ones
    who do not stick
    to what is realized already;
    they are the ones
    who know
    that all we have at the moment
    is nothing
    because it is not distributed very well.
    They are the hope
        and the future
        of the world.
Blessed are those
who suffer persecution
for the sake of justice,
for theirs is the kingdom of heaven.
    He was surrounded that day
    with people thinking of:
        "my eye"
        "my foot"

"my piles"
"my bowels"
"my nose"
"my toes."
They restricted themselves
to what they had.
They were not poor,
they were possessors.
They were unhappy.
They needed consolation.
But that day
he chose to speak to those
who did not possess
because of the lack of justice.
He chose to speak to those
who wept
and were meek
and merciful
and pure
and peace-making
and he said:
Hail to them,
hail,
they the blessed ones.
ARE YOU BLESSED
IN THIS WAY?

16.

RIOT IN THE TEMPLE

There is that report on a riot.
A report on a riot in the temple compound at Jerusalem.
The person who started the riot
was called Jesus.
Jesus,
a man coming from a sub-location,*
called Nazareth.
That Jesus entered the temple in the morning,
while the temple service was in full swing.
He is reported to have taken out his belt
and to have lashed out with it,
all around him.
Tables were turned over,
sacrificial animals were running all over the sacred place.
Sheep were squealing,
pigeons flew up from their cages,
and all kinds of money were rolling through the gutters
and over the pavement.
    It was quite a consternation,
    definitely a breach of peace,
    and everything happened so quickly,
    that the watchmen,
        the janitors,
        the temple askaris,†
        the doorkeepers and the police,
        did not even get the time
        to organize themselves.

*Sub-locations are the smallest administrative units in Kenya.

†African policemen, guards, or watchmen.

But that was not all.
An even worse thing happened
in that blessed compound,
in Jerusalem that day.
    But to understand this,
    we must remind ourselves of the fact,
    that you and I
    would not have been allowed to enter
    that temple area that day,
        because of our color,
        because of our religious convictions,
        and because of our background.
Animals were allowed to enter,
sheep were allowed to enter,
money was allowed to be brought in,
money from all the nations on the earth,
but the nations themselves,
and those who lived in those nations,
pagans and gentiles,
people like you and me,
they were not allowed to enter.
    The development that really caused consternation
    that day,
    was the fact that he,
    that upcountry Jesus,
    did not allow anyone
    to carry anything
    through the temple
    and over its square.
And that meant
that the temple service
was stopped.
All activity had come to an abrupt halt.
    Priests at the altar
    were looking for the next sacrificial animal,
    there was none;
    other priests were looking for the next person
    to be blessed,
    or to be purified,

there was nobody.
Priests, levites, scribes,
messengerboys, cleaners, sweepers,
and all the other assistants
could not believe their eyes:
Everything fell flat.
And there HE stood,
that Jesus from Nazareth,
once a refugee in Africa,
and he said,
no, of course he did not say it,
he shouted:
From now on
my house,
the house of my Father,
will be called
a house of prayer
FOR ALL NATIONS,
FOR ALL PEOPLE.
He, Jesus,
the Christ,
the Son of God,
suddenly broke through
that "apartheid"-barrier,
through all discrimination
and segregation,
and he pronounced
those divine words,
those divine words,
those divine words:
ALL AND EVERYBODY,
all men,
all men and women,
all nations,
all colors,
all cultures,
all,

    all,
    all,
    all,
    groups are out,
    they are out in justice,
    they are out in charity,
    they are out in worship,
    they are out.
He had done
and he had said this before
when he told his disciples,
so proud to belong to what they called
their INNER CIRCLE,
and so harsh against those
who wanted to join him,
keeping children and beggars away,
when he told those disciples,
who had asked him
how should we pray,
to say: OUR FATHER.
He had meant this before,
when he answered that woman in Samaria,
who asked him
how should we pray to God
on Mount Kirinyaga or on Mount Meru,*
that all those mountains were out,
and that from now on
all would have equal access to God,
in truth and in justice.
    He had meant this before when,
    while he was speaking
    somewhere in a social hall
    to a group of people,
    the doorkeeper came to warn him:

*Mount Kirinyaga is the vernacular name for Mount Kenya; Mount Meru is an extinct volcano in northeast Tanzania. Both mountains are considered sacred.

Your mother
and your brothers
and your sisters
are waiting outside
and when he said,
without even leaving the place
where he was standing:
My mother,
my brothers,
my sisters?
My family,
my family,
are these over here,
and everybody doing the will of God.
For him it was clear:
The whole of humankind is one family;
the whole of humankind should live in JUSTICE;
that is the foundation,
in justice, in brotherhood,
and in peace.
There is only one family,
the family of God,
the family of humankind.
Groups are out,
groups are dangerous,
groups are elitist,
groups are killers.
Apartheid is out,
things like Sharpeville,
where the whites shot
to kill the blacks
are completely out.
But the group-people
in that temple
that morning
in Jerusalem
did not forgive him

according to the report
  that came to us.
Those people
who had put at the entrance of the temple
those notes:
  HEBREWS ONLY,
they came together
in the corners
of that very same temple,
and they tried to find ways
to do away with him.
And they did away with him.
At least that is what they thought.
He died on the cross.
And they thought that in that way
they could do as well away
with that divine dimension:
ALL AND EVERYBODY.
  They were mistaken,
  he came back after his death,
  he won the battle,
  and we should be with him
  from all points of view,
  if we want to be Christians,
  and therefore as well
  from this point of view:
ALL AND EVERYBODY.

17.

THE PACT BETWEEN GOD AND THE POOR

In very many Old Testament readings
strangers are harassed,
orphans are trampled under feet,
widows are sucked empty,
   and the shouts of all those people
   cry to heaven,
   and the sky darkens because of them,
   and God wakes up;
   he listens to them,
   and thunder is heard,
   and lightning is prepared.
There seems to be a pact,
a hidden covenant,
a mysterious agreement,
a sacred oath,
   between God and the poor,
   between God and the lowly,
   between God and the needy,
   between God and the running noses of neglected children,
   between God and sore-inhabited heads,
   between God and the petrol-sniffers,
   between God and the empty-bellied ones.
There seems to be an arrangement,
a secret arrangement,
that he, God,
appears to us
through them,

that he, God,
appeals to us
 through that poor person
 through whose nose
 you can see,
 so to speak,
 with your permission,
 the worms in his bowels.
And with that Son of His,
Jesus of Nazareth,
God with us,
Emmanuel,
it was the same picture:
 The rich called on him,
 he bent over the poor;
 the learned Nicodemus made an appointment with him,
 after his working hours,
 he sat down with the children in the street;
 the pious Pharisees visited him,
 he had his meals with his fishermen friends;
 the important ones surrounded him,
 he stayed with the poor.
They asked him:
Who is the most important one?
and he took a child;
they asked him:
Who is my neighbor?
and he pointed at the beaten up stranger;
they asked him:
Do you like the temple?
and he said that he liked
the poor widow
who had just entered the door of that temple;
they asked him:
What should we eat?
and he broke his bread;
they asked him:
Only bread?

and he shared his fish;
they asked him:
What should we drink?
and he changed all the water
that they did not want to drink,
into very fine beer
they were very willing to drink;
they asked him:
How should we pray?
and he did not tell them:
   Pray like this,
   Father of Jesus . . .
He shared his Father with us,
and he told them:
   Pray like this,
   OUR Father . . .
They asked him:
What should we do?
and he said:
   You must love the Lord your God,
     that is the first thing;
    and you must love your neighbor,
     that is the second thing,
and then he added
in a kind of new kingdom mathematics:
   And those two
   are one.
They asked him:
What more should we do?
And he said:
   You must love yourself,
     that is the first thing,
    and your neighbor like yourself,
     that is the second thing,
and then he added
in a kind of new kingdom mathematics:
   And those two
   are one.

Behind all this,
there is his vision,
or,
if you want,
his theory,
his political working hypothesis,
or,
if you want,
his dream,
but a dream that is going to be turned
into reality.
It is his vision
of all people growing and hanging together
as one plant,
with one root,
with one stem
and one trunk,
with millions of connected seeds,
                    and flowers,
                    and leaves.
It is his theory,
of envisaging all people
as forming together
one body
with very many members,
with hands, feet, eyes, and ears,
and one life-spirit,
the holy one.
It is his dream
of seeing humankind forming
one people,
from all ages, all "races," all colors,
men and women,
young and old,
belonging together.
It is his belief
in one final get-together,
when the Father,

his Father and Our Father,
will call everybody from this world
and from the world of the dead,
for a final family reunion,
for the final get-together
of the family of God,
of the family of humankind.
   According to him,
   Jesus,
   we belong together,
   we should belong together.
   A belonging based on God's love,
   realizing God's love
   through us.
I should love you
as I love myself,
because we are destined
to be one
in Him.
You should love me
as you love yourself,
because we are meant
to be one in Him.
   This is a wide ideal,
   a superhuman humanitarian vision.
   The ideal is so lofty,
   that it does not mean so very much,
   in fact that it does not mean anything at all,
   until we break it down,
   as he broke it down,
      who received the rich,
      and bent over the poor;
      who had his theological appointment,
      and played with the children in the street.
We should break his vision down
in our charity,
in the fulfilment of our duties of state,
in our private budgeting,

in our political interests,
and in our personal considerations
   together with those
   and in favor of those
   who are near,
   who are the nearest,
   together with our neighbors.
And,
if this happens,
then the sky will clear up,
the lightning will be put away,
and God's blessing will descend
as gentle rain,
as dew in the morning,
on all of us.
   The country will change,
   and we will change,
   and the world will be a better one.
   And the result will be
   that
   in new kingdom mathematics,
   9,000,000,000 times person
   will be ONE.

18.

HOPELESS PESSIMISTS
AND
HOPELESS OPTIMISTS

Hope is important;
you cannot hope without faith.
Your faith is useless without hope.
Hope is not only a virtue;
hope is as well an abstraction.
It is something that does not exist.
Soap exists,
sugar exists,
salt exists,
you exist,
we exist,
but hope does not exist.
It only exists in a him
or in a her.
   So we must start
   with a him,
   or with a her,
   when speaking about hope.
Take Mr. Kamau.
Mr. Kamau is sick.
He is in great pains,
like so many in the world,
who are in great pains,
like so many in the gospels
who were in great pains.

Mr. Kamau,
who is sick,
can do different things.
He might say:
    I am beyond repair,
    it is no use,
    I am too old,
    worn out machinery,
    engine-knock,
    worn out organs,
    no servicing will help.
Mr. Kamau is a pessimist,
and he stayed at home
when Jesus passed his house.
The gospels have no report
on what happened
to those pessimists
because they stayed at home
when Jesus passed.
Mr. Kamau might react
in another way,
when being in great pains,
he might say:
    This happened before,
    I know what it is,
    it is going to pass
    it really is nothing serious.
    I will be all right.
    Tomorrow it will have passed,
    I do not need any help.
Mr. Kamau is an optimist.
He stayed at home
when Jesus passed his house.
The gospels have no report
on what happened
to those optimists
because they stayed at home
when Jesus passed.

Optimists and pessimists
are hopeless,
without hope;
they are self-centered,
they remain alone,
they do not go out,
they do not need anybody else;
there are no stories about them
in the whole of the four gospels.
The gospels are full of stories
about people in pains.
about people with
　　sore eyes,
　　lame legs,
　　internal bleedings,
　　stiff tongues,
　　deaf ears,
　　stupid heads,
　　and about people carrying
　　their dead with them.
They,
they left their homes;
they,
they came out of their hiding places;
they,
they were brought out of their rooms.
They came out,
or they were brought out,
because they hoped.
　　They were humble enough to do so.
　　Most probably they had done everything they could
　　to escape their fate.
　　But they had bumped against
　　the barriers of their impossibilities,
　　and they had recognized that fact.
　　They went out to somebody else,
　　they did not stay alone,
　　they asked for help,

they prayed for help,
they prayed hopefully,
they entered into communion
with somebody else,
they confided in him,
    and that is what hope
    is about,
    hope in a man,
    hope in a woman.
No egocentric optimism,
no egocentric pessimism,
    but a humble,
        trustful
        relating to someone,
        and communicating with that someone
        HOPEFULLY.
That is what makes
hope so difficult
to many of us.
We are too sure of ourselves,
we want to be too self-reliant;
we are optimists,
    and it is no help to be an optimist,
we are pessimists,
    and it is no help to be a pessimist.
We are very rarely really "hopeful,"
notwithstanding the possibilities we know of,
the possibility of going to Jesus,
the possibility of approaching
the Son of God,
the Maker of heaven and earth.

19.

WE ARE HIS MONEY

Today it is all about
a very popular subject:
It is all about money.
   There is the man with the 5,000 shillings,
   there is the man with the 2,000 shillings,
   and there is the man with the 1,000 shillings.
There is the man
who made out of his 5,000
another 5,000;
how he did it is not mentioned,
although it would be good to know.
There is the man
who made out of his 2,000
another 2,000,
and once more,
do not ask how,
because the Bible
does not give the answer
to that one.
   And there is the man
   who made nothing more
   out of his 1,000.
   He buried them,
   he did not even bury them in a bank,
   the best way,
   bankers say,
   to get rich while you sleep;
   although the bank,

I think,
will get richer still,
exactly because you are
asleep.
That last one buried his money
in his field,
where it did not sprout,
where it did not get roots,
where it did not grow.
And he is blamed.
Money, money, money,
and I would say,
money,
in a rather dirty way,
money only from the aspect
of making more money
and nothing else.
But I think
that everybody understands
that this story
must be about something else.
It is.
The story is about the end,
and about the account to be rendered
in the end.
And in the very end
money does not help.
You cannot take your money
with you;
you cannot take anything
with you
in the end.
That is even the reason
that many "experts" think
that in so many African traditions
people are completely undressed
before they are buried.

They go in
as they came out;
   all gain,
   all merit,
   all growth in between,
   must have been within
   within the walls of your skin,
   or it has not been.
You cannot take anything
but your own personality,
your own very self.
   Once I assisted
   at the deathbed of a very lucky farmer.
   He was so lucky,
   because he had lost his farm.
At first his farm
was in the open up-country.
But then a town started to grow,
first next to his shamba,*
then all around his shamba.
Suddenly he lived
with his sheep and his goats,
with his pigs and his hens
in the center of town.
Town bought him out,
and he got very, very much money.
   He liked all that money
   very, very much,
   and he built a safe
   in his sleeping-room,
   and in that safe
   he put all his money,
   and he considered not only that safe as safe,
   but he considered himself safe as well,
   safe and saved.

*Plot of ground under cultivation.

There he was
years later
on his deathbed
in that sleeping-room
with his safe
and all that money.
He realized he had to part;
he went to confession,
he received holy communion,
his extremities were anointed,
and then,
just before he died,
he felt for something under his pillow;
he brought something out,
nobody could see what it was,
a crucifix to be kissed?
a medal to be put on his chest?
It was the key to his safe;
he put it in his mouth,
and he swallowed it,
while he died.
It is not the money
that we take
with us;
it is ourselves,
our inner person.
    And it is that inner person
    that is compared with money too,
    but no longer with the money of people,
    but with the money of God.
Do you remember,
how once in the gospel,
the Pharisees,
trying to trap Jesus,
came with that question
about
paying your tax?

And how he asked them,
Show me the money,
and how they handed him a coin,
and how he asked,
Whose image does it bear?
Whose name is stamped in it?
   and they answered:
   It bears the image
   of the emperor
   and his name.
And how he then said:
   Give to the emperor,
   what is of the emperor.
And how he then said:
   And give to God
   what belongs to God.
He might have asked:
   Whose image do you bear,
   whose name is stamped in you?
And the answer would have been
or should have been:
   We are carrying God's image,
   we are carrying God's name.
He coined us
in his image,
he named us,
we are having
   his imprint,
   his stamp,
   his seal.
We are legal tenders
because of him.
We are his money,
and we should be spent,
that is the lesson of today.
   Money should circulate,
   we should circulate;
   money should go from hand to hand,

we should go from hand to hand;
money should be thumbed,
we should be thumbed;
money has to be used,
we have to be used;
money should get smudged in that process,
we should get smudged in that process;
money is going to be worn,
we should be going to be worn.
We should not keep ourselves
and all we've got
safe in a bank
or in an old cocoa-tin
or in an old sock
or under the sole of our shoes
or in the ivory tower of our competence
or under the cover of our dignity
or in the clenched fist of our power
or somewhere pinned under the bottom of a table:
    We should be spent,
    we are the coins,
    God is trying to use us,
    to pay off our debts,
    to pay off the debts we owe each other,
    here on earth,
    in Europe, in Portugal, in Angola,
    in Zimbabwe, in China, in Cuba,
    in the States, in Kenya, in Holland,
    all over the world.
Let us risk being used,
and we will be increased,
and the end will be glory,
because we made things better
for all the others
we lived and died with.

20.

SINS ARE THE TROUBLE

A man crawled up to Jesus,
on his knees,
with his clothing torn,
and his hair disordered,
shielding his upperlip
with his right hand,
shouting:
   Unclean,
   unclean;
all according to the prescriptions
of the old, old testament.
But between those words
imposed on him
by religious law,
  he whispered:
     If you want to
      you can cure me.
And he said:
Of course I want to,
and he touched him,
and his skin shook,
like in a skin-quake,
and the scabs fell off,
and the wounds closed,
and the swelling disappeared,
and the shiny spots,
they lost their shine.
  And Jesus said:
  Keep your mouth shut,
   do not tell the others.

That last remark
did not seem
very fair,
because
to keep his mouth shut
was exactly what that poor man
had been obliged to do
up to the moment
of his healing:
to keep his mouth shut
and to avoid contact,
living outside,
living apart,
with his hands over his lips,
shouting: Unclean.
　　He could not continue like that
　　and so he started,
　　he who had never been communicating before,
　　to communicate all over the place,
　　right,
　　left,
　　and center,
and the result was
that Jesus could no longer go openly
into any town,
that Jesus had to stay outside,
apart,
in places where nobody lived,
　　but that he did this
　　was not only to avoid the people
　　who flocked to him from all sides
　　when they saw him;
　　it was as well for another reason.
　　Those healings,
　　of course,
　　belonged to the picture,
　　they belonged to his work,
　　and yet,
　　yet,

was that
what he had come for?
Had he not come for all?
Had he not come
to change the whole situation?
Had he only come to oil
the inedible circumstances
of some?
You must have heard
about a man
called Frantz Fanon.
He had a clinic in North Africa;
he was a psychiatrist,
treating mentally disturbed North Africans,
or in gospel terms:
chasing away bad and evil spirits.
    He did this until 1956,
    then he stopped,
    and he left the clinic
    where he had been working,
    because he had come to the insight
    that it was useless
    to work on sick individuals only,
    that it would be much more useful
    to work on the situation,
    the human situation as such at that time
    in the North Africa of that time,
    that made people sick,
    because they did not feel at home
    in their own colonized country,
    and he became a politician,
    fighting with the rebels,
    and he wrote a letter
    to the Minister of Health
    to explain his decision.
Jesus must have understood
that all the sicknesses,
and especially all those evil spirits,

he was facing all around him,
were born from within,
from within the more general human situation,
a situation
that was sick and sinful,
alienating and oppressive,
    and that is why he preferred
    to attack that more general human condition
    when he cleansed
    or tried to cleanse
    the temple-service;
    when he condemned and criticized the leaders
    but as well their followers;
    when he was redemptive to all,
    and when he told the people he healed
    before he even touched them:
        Your sins are forgiven,
        because those sins
        are the real trouble,
        the injustice,
        the neglect,
        the untamed passions,
        the greed,
        the drinking,
        the fornicating,
        the meanness,
        and the cowardice.
Sometimes,
very often in fact,
we hear Jesus say
in the gospel-reports
to a man or a woman:
        Your sins are forgiven.
        He said it,
        for example,
        to that man
        who was lowered
        through the roof

in front of him
at his feet:
Your sins are forgiven.
And I think
that almost all of us
are then conditioned
in such a way
that we think
that he meant
to forgive
the sins of the man
in front of him.
But is that necessarily true?
Would it not be possible,
no, even probable,
that Jesus meant:
    Your sins,
    all the sins that made you sick,
    whether they are committed
    by you
    or by others
    all those sins
    are forgiven,
    and that is why I can add now:
    Take up your bed and walk.
Not his sins
but sins made him sick.
Not my sins
but sins make me sick.
    Let me give you an example.
    I know a boy over here in town,
    who is, I think,
    mentally sick,
    that is to say,
    he is in that type
    of state,
    that the people around Jesus
    would have interpreted

as being possessed.
People over here
in town
tried to help that boy:
    They registered him in a school,
    he gave up;
    they registered him
    in another school;
    he gave up,
    he, barely twelve years old,
    sold his shoes,
    his uniform,
    his blanket,
    and he bought a knife.
    Where does that evil spirit come from?
    Why did he buy a knife?
    Why is he sniffing petrol?
        When his father died,
        his mother left him,
        nobody cared;
        he had to fend
        for himself alone.
        And the society,
        the society we live in,
        left him alone.
And all those sins,
his sins,
her sins,
society's sins,
your sins,
and my sins
left in this boy
a residue,
a remainder,
an inert rest,
that functions like an evil spirit,
and that makes
that small boy,

growing up amongst us,
ravingly mad:
 And all those sins
 should be forgiven,
 before anything will happen,
 and we should recreate
 our structures
 in such a way
 that things like this
 should not happen anymore.
Jesus healed the sick,
he chased away evil spirits,
he attacked the results of our bad society
at that level,
 but he attacked it as well
 elsewhere
 in society,
 by attacking that society,
 not only there where individuals went wrong,
 but there where society itself went wrong,
 politically and otherwise.
 And if we want,
 do we really want?
 But if we really want
 to participate
 in his redemptive work
 we too should do the same.
 So that all may be saved.

21

NINE PLUS ONE MAKES TEN

There is that story
about the ten lepers.
They were a very mixed crowd,
Jews and a Samaritan.
Misery had brought them together,
misery and the law
ruling and checking their misery.
They were all recognized lepers,
genuine ones,
and therefore all
outcasts.
    They came to meet Jesus,
    that man who was causing
    change and renewal
    all around himself.
    They were carefully sticking to the rules;
    that is why they remained
    standing some way off,
    as prescribed.
    Everything was prescribed for them,
    they knew exactly what to do
    and what not to do,
    they kept strictly to the rules
    of a leper's life.
Although,
now,
now they were asking for something

out of the booklet;
they were asking to be healed.
   And he heals them,
   of course he heals them,
   he tells them
   to take up their normal
   pre-leprosy life again,
   he tells them
   to show themselves to the priests,
   to undergo the very complicated
   and the very costly purification rites,
   with birds and lambs,
   oil, water, scarlet,
   and all kinds of other strange goings-on.
They all go
and do exactly as they were told
on the way to their normal healthy lives,
the life they had to interrupt
when becoming a leper.
They are happy to be like the others
again,
happy, grateful, and quite satisfied.
   But then
   something happens
   in one of them;
   he suddenly realizes
   what overcame him,
   and he returns,
   shouting at the top of his voice,
   and he throws himself
   at the feet of Jesus.
   But nothing
   seems ever to have been heard
   from the others.
Those others returned
   to the temple,
   to the church,
   to their homes,

to their work,
to their normal activities
as if nothing
      nothing
had happened.
They were touched by Jesus,
they were touched in their bodies,
they were touched in their desires,
and they disappeared.
In fact hardly anything
seemed to have taken place.
Next day they were selling their wares in their shops,
writing their ciphers in their books,
and the following holy day
they went to worship
in the temple.
   A strange story,
   a strange riddle,
   a strange parable,
   a strange example.
We are Christians,
we are baptized,
confirmed,
we receive his body and blood,
we are touched much more,
much more intensely
than any of those ten lepers.
After all, leprosy is a surface,
a skin disease.
We are deeper touched,
deeper healed,
deeper saved.
   But who do we resemble,
   the nine who disappeared
   into normal life,
      nicely,
      snugly,
      morally,

quietly,
ecclesiastically,
law-abidingly,
or the one,
who could not hold himself,
who suddenly understood
what had happened to him:
being touched by the Lord,
being touched by the divine,
and who started to cry
at the top of his voice,
taking a third chance?
>   His first chance had been
>   not to believe at all
>   and remain sick
>   and unhealed;
>   he did not take that chance,
>   it was not even so much of a chance.
>   His second chance was
>   to be healed
>   and to return to normal life,
>   to forget about it,
>   and to be normal
>   as all the others
>   as the nine others did.
>   But he took a third chance:
>   to admit that something
>   terrific had happened
>   and to return to his healer
>   and to throw himself at his feet,
>   to thank him for the new liberty
>   and to live accordingly.
One out of ten,
or perhaps better,
one out of ten times only
we are like that Samaritan.
Nine out of ten times

we are just like all the others
in our church,
that became like a firm,
a very old
and a very well-established firm,
dealing in
   liturgics,
   oil,
   water,
   bread,
   and a sacred lamb.
A church
in which we are
most of the time
in the company of those nine,
the normal ones,
the citizens.
   Let us allow
   ourselves
   now and then,
   and more and more,
   to run away from it,
   to shout at the top of our voices,
   to indulge in the new liberty
   given to us
   and the new vision
   opened to us,
   and to fall at his feet
   and to be like
   number ten.

22.

THE GOOD, THE BAD, AND THE STUPID

We all are trying
over here in this chapel
to form a Christian community,
a Catholic one.
We try to worship
in the way Jesus worshipped,
Jesus who called God his Father,
and who,
as a logical consequence,
considered all men and women
as the offspring from that Father,
and therefore as his brothers and sisters.
And that is why he,
Jesus,
in the midst of that very extended family
of his,
    took his bread,
        his fish,
        his wine,
        his salt,
        his oil,
        his light,
        his healing power,
        his wisdom,
        his experience,
        and his life
        to break it

and to share it
    with all.
He, Jesus,
he had a vision,
he had a dream,
that once we all would be with the Father.
We,
his followers,
should share in that vision,
we should share in that dream
or whatever you would like
to call it:
    faith,
    belief,
    trust,
    hope,
    commitment,
    philosophy,
    or being saved.
    I do not care so much
    what you call it,
    as long as you share it.
There is a gospel reading
in which Jesus himself
works this out.
It is when he tells
about the reaction
of different people
invited to the table of his Father.
Just as we,
who are now busy with
    our studies,
    our farms,
    our businesses,
    our love-affairs,
    our children,
    our oxen,
    our goats,

    our boom,*
    our meal vouchers,†
    our accommodation problems,
    our struggles,
    our frustrations,
    our helplessness,
    our big mouths,
    and our small hearts,
are,
in the final instance,
invited to something else,
to something more,
to a heavenly wedding feast,
to a final outcome,
to a putting together of all the pieces,
to an ultimate graduation day.
We too are invited
to realize
    that behind
    or beyond all this,
    that through and in all this
    a new life is going to be born.
The people invited
in Jesus' story
reacted in different ways:
    There were the ones
    that did not come;
    they were not interested,
    they did not see,
    they were too busy;
        one went up to his farm,
        to count his cattle
        and his coffee plants;
        another one
        went to his shop in town,

---

*The name the students use for their money allowance.

†Tickets used to obtain meals from the university kitchens.

to count his shillings
and his bags of hoarded sugar,
and others went even so far
as to harass
the messengerboys
who came with the invitation cards.
They did not see,
they were the dim ones,
they were the stupid ones;
nothing is heard about them
any more.
But then there were
the good ones
that came
because they saw;
and then there were
the bad ones
that came
because they too saw.
And the king came in,
entering the hall,
and he looked around,
and he was happy,
very happy,
that there were so many
to honor his son,
who was going to marry,
because that wedding was the occasion
of his invitation.
And the king sat down,
and he took a glass,
and a piece of roasted meat,
and he put on his eyeglasses,
because kings do not wear specs,
they wear eyeglasses,
and he looked around,
and what did he do?

Did he kick out the good ones?
Of course he did not kick out
the good ones.
Did he kick out the bad ones?
He did not kick out the bad ones.
He only kicked out
that one,
that one
who had slipped in
without an appropriate dress.
He had come with the others,
but the others had believed in the feast,
they had seen the vision.
He,
the one who was going to be kicked out,
had come with them,
but he had not believed
that there really would be a feast,
and not believing that,
he had not prepared himself for it either.
He had no vision,
and he was thrown out
in the dark,
where people without vision belong,
because they do not see,
together with the others,
who had not even come.
Should we then
condemn the dim, the stupid ones?
Should we even call
or be allowed to call those without vision
the dim, the stupid ones?
   I think that God might do that,
   I think that Jesus might do that,
   but we?
   If we stress too much
   that others do not see,

we might be condemning ourselves,
who maintain that we see.
We should share the vision of Christ,
who called God his Father,
and therefore all people
his brothers and his sisters,
and who took as a consequence of that vision
his bread,
his fish,
his wine,
his salt,
his light,
his oil,
his power,
his wisdom,
his experience,
and his life
to break and share it
with all.
We see,
because he *did* that.
Would it not be possible,
that others would see,
if we would *do*
as he did.
What about me,
and I,
I shudder.
What about you,
do you shudder too?

23.

FRIEND AND SEX

They were on the point
of hurling their stones,
rocks and dirt,
to break her,
to crack her,
to kill her,
and to show
how bad she was,
and how just and good they were,
the defenders of morals
and of God,
of law and order.
   AND JESUS SAID:
     Will anyone without sin
      please show me his identity card,
      so that I can check.
Speaking about adultery,
we are speaking about sex,
and when we speak about sex
we often understate
its importance in human life.
When we speak about sex
we think about
   ears,
   noses,
   wet mouths,
about
   legs,
   breasts,

    hips,
    shoulders,
and all kinds of other
    anatomical items,
    that are so nicely drawn out
    in full
    on lavatory walls
    and study-desks
    all over the world:
    kingsize,
    olympic measures.
And even in confessional boxes
we tend to restrict ourselves
to what we then
rather strangely call:
    dirty desires,
    dirty thoughts,
    dirty acts,
    lusting after man
    or woman.
Is that all
that can be said
about sex?
    Great authors
    and artists,
    great men
    and great women,
    in all ages,
    in all regions,
    speak differently.
They say
that a man
who is knocking at the door
of a woman
is not only looking for her,
and the woman
who opens so eagerly the door
is not only longing for him.

They are both looking for far more:
   for salvation,
   for redemption,
   for fulfillment,
   for a companion,
   for a neighbor,
   for a friend,
   for ourselves.
It is no good to be alone;
it is Eve who gave Adam
his name;
it is Adam who gave Eve
her name.
We are unfair to ourselves
when we think
that sex
is only
sex.
   Sex is part and parcel
   of much more,
   of ourselves;
   it is part of our quest
   for ourselves
   and even for immortality:
      A person
      who marries
      overcomes death
      according to so many
      African proverbs.
It is at the moment
that we forget this,
it is at the moment
that we do not take sex
seriously,
or that we do not take it
in its full context,
that sin creeps in:
because that type of sex

is a lie;
it does not liberate,
it arrests,
it binds,
it enslaves.
 You all know the story
 of that beautiful girl,
 so beautiful,
 who was deceived by a man,
 a man,
 a sugar-daddy,
 who told her:
  I am going to open the world to you;
  I am going to make you great
  in the eyes of all the others;
  I am going to show you
  who you really are;
  I am going to introduce you
  to life, to real, real life.
And the only thing he did
was to undress her,
to unwrap her,
and to take her,
afterwards going his way.
 What a shame,
 what a waste,
 what a deception,
 what a sin,
 what a scandal,
 what a mockery,
 what a mistake.
And the father of that woman
and the fathers of all women,
the mother of that woman
and the mothers of all women
 hide their heads in shame
 that a man could behave like that,
 without any respect.

The crowd was approaching Jesus.
The police became nervous.
There were shouts,
obscene words,
they were dragging somebody along;
they stopped before him,
sitting there to teach the crowds.
    The group of shouters opened up
    and a woman fell out.
    They told her to stand up,
    to stand on top of that step
    over there,
    and they looked at Jesus
    and they said:
        What about her,
        we caught her with a stranger?
    What about that man?
    What about that man?
    Where was that man?
Jesus did not look up;
he played with some sand,
some sand in his hand.
They insisted,
and then he said:
    If anyone is without sin
    among you,
    let him throw the first stone.
And he played with some sand,
some sand in his hand.
    And everybody left,
    the oldest ones first,
    they are the worst.
And he looked at the woman:
    Had she been looking for salvation,
    for redemption,
    for fulfillment,
    for a companion,
    for a neighbor,

for a friend,
for herself?
And he said:
    Where are they,
    has no one condemned you?
And she said:
    No, sir.
And he said:
    I am not going to do that either,
    go,
    and do not sin anymore.
And at that moment
she found
everything she had been looking for:
    a savior,
    a redeemer,
    fulfillment,
    a companion,
    a neighbor,
    a friend.
A friend
who forgave the past,
who respected her,
who did not condemn her,
but who said:
    Do not sin any more,
    do not look for liberation
    in the wrong place.
    Go away,
    get organized,
    start a new life,
    a more human life,
    a more liberated life.
He left it to her,
that is really him.
He leaves it to us,
that is really him.
But he adds,

the promise
and the assurance
   of a better self,
   of a better you,
   of a better me,
   of a new person.

24.

UNCORRUPT JUDGES

It sometimes seems
that the gospel is against
judging.
We should not turn ourselves into judges.
We should not make distinctions
between classes of people.
Judgments and distinctions
should be left to God.
And the gospel indicates
how his judgment works:
    He opens the eyes of the blind
    and the ears of the deaf;
    he loosens the tongues of the mute
    and the legs of the lame;
    he does justice to the poor
    and to the oppressed;
    he gives bread to the hungry
    and drink to the thirsty;
    he protects the stranger
    and the widows and the orphans;
    or to sum it up:
    God heals all the damage done to this world,
    God heals all the damage done to people,
    damage not caused by him,
    damage caused by people,
    damage done by me,
    damage done by you,
    damage done by the old and by the young.

The gospel texts
do not ask
not to judge.
They do not forbid us to be critical.
If we are not critical,
if we do not judge,
how is this world going to change?

    How are the poor
    and the sick
    and the hungry
    and the squatters
    and the naked
    and the landless
    and the strangers
    and the orphans
    and the thirsty
    and the unemployed
    and the exploited
    and the widows
    and the prostitutes
    and the dropouts
    and you
    and me
    going to survive,
    if we do not judge?

The gospels are not against judging;
they are against a certain type of judging.
They are against superficial judging;
they are against corrupt judging;
they are against false judging.
They indicate very clearly
what they are against.

    There is the example of the rich man,
    well fed,
    golden-ringed,
    beautifully dressed,
    highly perfumed,

who comes in
with a nice smile
and a fat wallet,
with a curl in his hair
and a flower in his buttonhole
and with new shoes cracking under him,
and the priest
and the sacristan
and the others,
they run up
to greet him
and to give him
the best place.
   And then a second man comes in,
   hungry looking,
   hardly dressed,
   rather smelly,
   with a string around his waist,
   with some grass and hay in his hair
   and his toes sticking out of his shoes,
and the priest
and the sacristan
and all the others,
they rush up
to park him in a corner
on the floor,
so that the first one
will not be hindered
by the smell
of number two.
   And that although
   the judgment of God
   helps the poor,
   respects the hungry,
   and heals all damage done.
I know a man,
a rather poor man,

and for that reason not so very much
appreciated by others,
who saves every penny
he can save,
sometimes it takes him a year,
to be able to hire a car
for a full day,
once a year.
He then takes the biggest Mercedes-Benz
he can find,
from around the corner over here
at University Road,
and drives it.

When you close the door
of such a car,
you hear a bang,
a dazzling bang,
a terrific bang,
a mile around.
One of the things
of such a car
is that impressive bang.
If you have a small car,
you only hear an insignificant
bing,
a very tiny and a very tinny noise,
as if you are opening a bottle of beer,
or a can with fish in tomato sauce.

The bang of a Mercedes is different;
when that bang is heard,
policemen
take roadblocks away;
security people salute;
hotelkeepers almost fall over
and praise the Lord.
Waiters and doorkeepers
rush on,
servants put their dresses straight

and start to roll their eyes.
There he is,
the bang,
the big monumental bang.
   He rents it,
   that big car,
   for one day,
   to be respected
   for that one day.
There were two friends,
older parish priests,
somewhere in the west.
They decided to test
the judging
of their colleagues
in the light of the gospel texts.
They grew beards
for a few days,
they put on old clothing
and old shoes,
they left their hair uncombed,
their face unwashed,
and they put old bags
over their shoulders,
after having filled them
with some rags.
And they started to go
from door to door
at the houses of their colleagues,
the parish priests.
   They knocked at the doors of friends,
   friends they had been discussing with
   some evening before
   about charity and justice,
   about kindness and the poor
   and other things like that.
   Priests they knew very well
   opened doors they knew very well.

They asked for a sleeping place
and they got only some cents.
They asked for a meal,
something to eat,
and the doors closed in their faces.
Once they were received in a kitchen;
a maidservant had opened the door.
They got some leftovers,
a bit of kindness,
but then
their colleague and friend
the parish priest came in.
He did not recognize them
in his anger;
he kicked them out,
and while they were leaving
they heard him shout
to spray the chairs
on which they had been sitting
with insecticide.
They were not welcome,
far from it.
It is that type of judging
the gospels forbid
as being corrupt.
It is that judging that is
undivine,
superficial,
uncharitable,
and damaging.
In our judging
we should try
to judge like God,
in a healing way,
in an effectively healing way:
Your roommate who drinks
or smokes bang;
your fellow student who is frustrated

or so terribly homesick;
your colleague who is scared stiff
because of the examinations
and who isolates himself so strangely;
your blind companion
who trips
and asks for help
while queuing up
at the end of the line
at the catering unit.*
That is how we should judge
the ignorant around us,
the oppressed,
and the sick.
  Let us judge each other
  in a healing way,
  not in a damaging way,
  not like corrupt judges.
    Let us judge,
    covering up,
    making up
    for the damage done to us,
    for the damage done by us.

*Dining hall.

25.

AN OLD CLOAK AND
A LIVING HEART

There is that story about an old cloak;
in that time it could not have been
about an old pair of trousers,
they did not wear them.
There was that old cloak.
It was so dear to its owner
or so indispensable
because he had only one
that he repairs it.
  He buys a piece of cloth,
  new and unshrunk,
  not even pre-shrunk,
  and he sews it carefully
  on that old cloak of his.
  When the piece is put on,
  he puts the whole lot
  in water to be washed;
  he hangs it over a drying line,
  and in the sun
  the new patch shrinks
  and the old material does not.
  He puts his cloak on,
  and the very first time
  that he bends to have a look
  at his shoes
  or his toes,

he hears a tear
and the new piece falls off.
And all this
seems to have very much to do
with one of the most discussed
theological issues
in Africa.
It is the discussion
on the relation
between the old and the new.
   African authors like Okot p Bitek,
   Ngugi wa Thiongo, Taban lo Liong,
   Wanjala, Ochieng, Micere Mugo,
   and Mbula, do not open their mouths,
   or unscrew their pens
   without speaking about it.
   And they speak about it
   exactly in the way
   the gospel story
   of that old cloak does.
They all point at their societies
in the central province,
in the western province,
in the eastern province,
or in the northern province,
and they say:
   Christianity
   tore up those societies;
   Christianity broke them down.
James Mburu, Sarah Kabetu,
and so many others
have been describing how
Christianity
broke the backbone
of the old set-up,
and how the new piece
made the tear worse.

And I think
that there is much truth
in all they say.
Missionaries very often
did not know what they were doing,
but I think as well
that we can see now
what went wrong
and what we can do about it.
   Saint Paul
   gives us another model
   to think about the relation
   old and new.
   He does not use the model
   of a cloak or of a pair of trousers,
   of old and new things.
   Saint Paul wrote
   that he did not write
   the new message,
   the new spirit,
   in things
   or in tablets of stone.
   He wrote
   in living hearts.
A cloak is a thing,
an old pair of trousers is a thing,
an old shirt is a thing,
a piece of cloth is a thing,
a gallon of wine is a thing,
and the skin in which you put it
is a thing;
   if you force a thing,
   it breaks,
   it cracks,
   it tears off,
   it splits open;
   things do not give way,
   things cannot give way.

But we are not things,
our societies are not things,
our traditions are not things:
    We are alive,
    we are living,
    and as we are alive
    we cannot do very much
    with that example of that cloak.
One of the mistakes
those missionaries must have made,
because we Christians make that mistake
so often ourselves,
one of those mistakes must have been
that they treated themselves
and the others as things,
as non-living things.
    Take that man,
    that older man,
    married with more than one,
    in fact with many wives,
    and who wants to become a Christian,
    and the priest
    or the catechist
    tells him:
    No new patch
    on that old cloak of yours;
    no new wine in that old skin of yours,
    no new wine in the un-Christian set-up,
    no new wine in your old relationships:
    Choose one,
    take one,
        and let your feet
        not carry you anymore,
        to house two,
        to house three,
        to house four,
        to house five.
What about those wives,

what about their children,
what about the whole set-up?
   What to do?
   What to do?
   What to do?
In another letter,
the one to the Romans,
Saint Paul wrote
   that every human culture,
   that every human civilization,
   that every traditional human attempt
   to organize life and survival,
   should be seen
   as a living branch,
   as a living shoot,
   as a living graft
   on the fundamental root JESUS.
All cultures,
wrote Paul,
should be grafted on that root,
to share its rich sap,
the rich juice,
the Spirit flowing over in the branches,
so that they are going to be changed,
transformed,
slowly
but surely
bringing forth fruits
plenteously.
And even that kind of strange
hybrid modern culture
in which most of us are living nowadays
should be grafted on him,
on that root,
to change
slowly but seriously
   and even that culture
   will not fall off.

26.

THE KINGDOM IS IN

To be a Christian on this Nairobi campus
is not something dead
or a mere idea
or a vague perspective
or an abstract category
or a false, unrealistic
psychological dimension.
   It is something real,
   something very involving.
   Some time ago,
   a student came in,
   late at night,
   knocking at the door.
   He came in,
   he sat down,
   and he talked about nothing,
      and again about nothing,
      and finally about something.
Two of his friends were,
he thought,
at a loss.
They were making pots
and weaving baskets,
because they thought
that the kingdom of God
was very near.
   They thought that it was only
   a question of a few weeks,
   and then Christ would return

and claim this world;
the kingdom would come
with all its gifts.
He was going to descend to earth,
and they wanted to be ready,
with their pots and their baskets,
to receive him
and his gifts.
Jesus was going to come,
alleluia, brother,
alleluia, sister,
alleluia, plants,
alleluia, animals,
alleluia, everybody.
      And then a Christian newspaper
      added an extra feature
      to its *Target*,*
      very well prepared,
      very impressive,
      very well documented,
      indicating as well
      that the end of these sinful times
      is very,
      very near.
      The world was almost at its end;
      all the signs were there:
            the floods,
            the droughts,
            the wars,
            the starvations,
            the upheavals,
            the dangers to Israel.
The new creation
was going to start
any time from now,
they were almost counting down:

Target is an East African Christian newspaper that published
a twelve-page supplement on the threatening end of the world.

ten weeks,
nine weeks,
eight weeks,
six weeks,
seven days,
three days,
two hours,
twenty-one seconds,
twenty seconds,
nineteen,
eleven,
eight,
six,
almost
now.
And yet
all this seems very strange.
Because if you really listen
to that kingdom prophet
JESUS OF NAZARETH,
as well called,
the blessed one,
you might start to wonder
whether he thought about that kingdom
like that.

    Has it still to come?
    Is it not yet here?
    Is it still over there?
    He said:
        The kingdom is like a seed,
        already put in the soil;
        it is like yeast
        working in the dough;
        it is like the ferment
        that makes the beer bubble;
        it is like a treasure
        hidden in the field;
        it is like a pearl

that is found;
like fish
caught in the net.
That is his theory about the kingdom.
But is that true,
is the kingdom really
here already,
is it really in us?
   If it is,
   it should be traceable,
   verifiable.
   It must be possible to test
   his theory.
Let us test it.
It seems clear
what the kingdom of God is about.
It is about
   peace,
   justice,
   human dignity,
   equality,
   charity,
   liberty,
   and respect.
In all these fields
we have our ideas, norms, and ideals.
When we judge others,
we judge them according
to those principles,
the principles of the kingdom.
We say:
   He should never have treated his girl friend
   like that,
   and we decide that we should not treat her
   like that
   either.
We say:
   It is a scandal that he used his position

to bribe and to deceive,
and we decide that we should not
bribe and deceive in such a position
either.
We say:
    That administrator should have been
    more understanding
    and we decide that we too should be
    more understanding.
We judge
and we judge continually
according to the principles,
the principles of the kingdom.
    We gnash our teeth
    when the kingdom is not realized;
    we are full of joy
    when we notice its growth.
Indeed,
the kingdom of God is in,
    it is in us,
    it is in you,
    it is in me,
    it is in all:
    a hidden treasure,
    a forgotten pearl,
    a fish still in the water,
    but already caught;
    the yeast,
    or spirit,
    pushing up the dough,
    alleluia.

27.

WE ARE THE HOLY PLACE

We are here, this morning,
in a chapel,
in a church,
in a temple.
    It is a holy place,
    it is the house of God.
    That is why we are full of reverence:
    We crossed ourselves,
    we knelt down,
    we do not speak any more,
    we act as if we do not know each other;
    friends are sitting next to each other
    as strangers;
    mothers hardly seem to recognize
    their children;
    eyes are closed,
    knees are bent,
    noses are controlled,
    throats are checked,
    and even if we sit,
    we sit more solemnly than elsewhere:
        May you cross your legs
        while sitting in a temple?
When speakers are invited over here
a hesitation seems to creep
into their minds:
        May we say what we think
        about sex
        in a temple?

    May I speak about my difficulties
    with Christ
    or his missionaries
    in this,
    his house?
This is a holy place,
this is a temple;
and we the disciples of Jesus,
because that is what we are,
we are full of holy fear,
just like his disciples in Jerusalem
when they saw that temple
over there.
They said:
    Look how nice,
        how beautiful;
    look at the stones,
    look at the wood,
    look at the metals used,
    holy, very holy.
But Jesus said:
    This temple is nothing,
    it is nothing,
    nothing,
    nothing,
    nothing.
    I am going to do away with it,
    I am going to destroy it,
    I am going to show you
    the real temple of God,
    the real temple of God on this earth:
    PEOPLE,
    it is you,
    it is me,
    it is us.
There are no holy places,
there are no holy times,
there are no holy buildings.

ONE ONLY IS HOLY:
GOD,
and PEOPLE IN WHOM GOD DWELLS.
　　You remember the story about Jacob;
　　his father was dying;
　　Jacob wanted to be blessed;
　　he wanted to get the best possible blessing
　　from his father.
　　His mother Rebecca helped him;
　　she emptied Esau's wardrobe,
　　she stole his clothing,
　　and she put it on Jacob,
　　her favorite son;
　　she even stole Esau's smell
　　and made Jacob smell like him.
And Jacob got the blessing,
the very best one,
the one that was destined
for his brother,
Esau,
by fraud,
by lies,
by deception.
　　When Esau heard this,
　　he swore:
　　I am going to kill Jacob,
　　as soon as my father is dead.
　　Rebecca, their mother, overheard him,
　　and she told Jacob,
　　her favorite son,
　　get away,
　　your brother Esau
　　is trying to kill you.
So Jacob got away
in a hurry,
on his way to an uncle,
he did not even know:
Laban.

It became dark,
night fell;
Jacob,
not very much of an adventurer,
got afraid,
but finally decided to look
for a place to sleep.
He was lonely,
an outlaw,
unprotected,
without support,
and in fact with a prize on his head.
He found a place,
and he took a stone
to put under his head,
and he fell asleep.
　　He got a dream;
　　he saw a ladder reaching into heaven,
　　angels climbing up and down,
　　and God himself appearing
　　and telling him:
　　Be sure that I am with you,
　　I will keep you safe
　　wherever you go,
　　and I will bring you back,
　　wherever you went.
And Jacob woke up,
full of awe,
and when wide awake
he made a strange mistake:
He said:
Truly God is in this place,
and I never knew it,
this is the house of God.
　　And he took the stone;
　　he had slept his head upon,
　　and he put it up straight;
　　he poured oil over it,

and he consecrated the place,
giving it a new name;
up to then it was called Luz;
but he gave it the name BETHEL,
that is:
HOUSE OF GOD.
How strange,
what a logic!
He saw God in a dream,
so he saw God in himself,
    in his mind,
    in his heart,
    in his liver,
    or wherever we have our dreams.
    He could have fallen asleep
    in another place,
    in another region,
    in another land,
    with the same mind,
                    heart,
                    and liver;
and yet he said:
This PLACE is holy;
and he did not say:
I AM HOLY.
This chapel is not the holy place,
this temple is not the holy place.
Jesus said:
I am going to do away with it,
I am going to build a new temple,
not made of stones
or wood
or metal,
but of PEOPLE.
It is people
who are the temple of God.
All respect
due to the temple

is due to people,
to ourselves,
to each other:
We are the carriers of God
in this world.
      And that is why
      it is very serious
      when we are knocked over our heads,
      òr when we are knocking others
      over their heads;
      that is why it is very serious
      when people starve
      or have to drink dirty water
      or live in hopeless housing
      or get blind
      because nobody cares about the flies
      in their eyes.
            They,
            we
            are the temple of God.

28.

PETER AND PAUL

Saint Peter and Saint Paul
are always celebrated together.
That is strange,
not only because
even much less important Christian ancestors
have their own private and personal feast days,
but as well because Saint Peter and Saint Paul
had difficult times in each other's company;
    they discussed,
    they dialogued,
    they fought,
    they avoided each other for days and days,
    and then again faced each other
    in power and force.
Yet it is good,
I think,
that we celebrate them together,
because Saint Peter and Saint Paul
kept each other in balance,
in a very necessary balance.
    Saint Peter was the churchman,
    the typical churchman;
    Jesus called him the rock,
    the stone,
    on which the community
    was going to be built,
    but he might have called him
    as well
    the rock or the stone

because of Peter's tendency
to solidify,
to petrify.
Peter wanted safety
and a well-protected house.
Think of his attitude
on that mountain top
when in front of Peter's eyes
Jesus changed,
developed,
transfigured, glorified.
Elijah appears,
Moses appears,
and Jesus speaks to them
about what he is going to do;
he is talking about his passover,
about a new life,
and Peter says:
    Stop,
    keep it,
    hold it,
    this is super,
    alleluia,
    let us build something around it,
    let us keep it safe and warm,
    within walls under a roof.
Peter the rock,
the brick-and-stone believer,
the churchman, the builder, the contractor.
And then Saint Paul,
the exact opposite.
When Peter tried to close the doors
to the uncircumcised
and people like that,
Paul threw them open again.
When Peter insisted:
    Law, law,
    order, order,

Saint Paul wrote about
   the glorious liberty of the children of God,
   and he wrote:
   Where the spirit of God is, there is freedom;
   and he even added
   a thing very rarely quoted by churchleaders:
   "Why should freedom depend on
   somebody else's conscience";
   and in his difficulties with Saint Peter
   he shouted:
      Liberty, brothers,
      liberty, sisters,
      you are called to liberty.
Peter and Paul,
they keep each other in balance.
With Peter alone we would be a rock.
With Paul alone we would be an open door.
But both worked,
notwithstanding their difficulties,
with the same vision,
and both of them
got that vision
from Jesus himself,
be it in very different ways.
   Paul got his like this:
   He was sitting on a horse,
   fiery as ever,
   a kind of spiritual cowboy,
   with his sheriff-star under his lapel
   and in his pocket a list of names
   of the people he was going to arrest.
   Just normal names
   of people in Damascus and the environment,
   a list of the local
      Kamaus,
      Otienos,
      Agesas,

Odhiambos,
    and Wanjikus.*
He was going to arrest them
and to bring them to court
because they were subversive.
They were spreading rumors
about a resurrection from the dead,
about an ascension to heaven,
about a new way to be taken,
about the end of an old world order,
about an axe at the root of the old tree of life,
and about other items like that.
Paul was out,
as the Acts of the Apostles say,
to *slaughter* them.
    There he was on his horse
    in a hurry,
    because he wanted to arrive
    before the news of his coming
    could have arrived,
    to be able to take them by surprise.
And suddenly
there was that light
all around him,
and his horse fell,
and he fell,
and he heard a voice,
a voice that said:
    Saul, why are you persecuting ME?
    And Saul thought about the names on his list:
    the Kamaus,
    the Otienos,
    the Agesas
    the Odhiambos,
    and the Wanjikus;

*Common Kenyan names.

and he said:
    You,
    who are you?
  And the voice said:
    I am Jesus.
And Paul was very surprised,
because that name
was not on his list.
That man Jesus
was exactly the one
  who was rumored to have been executed,
  and risen,
  and ascended into heaven.
But then suddenly
he started to understand
that that Jesus
identified himself with those
  Kamaus,
  Otienos,
  Agesas,
  Odhiambos,
  and Wanjikus.
He got his vision,
there and then,
and he declared afterward:
  Jesus is the Head,
and we
are the members.
He got his vision,
the vision of Jesus.
  Peter got that vision,
  that very same vision,
  in another way.
  Jesus asked:
    Peter, do you love ME?
  Peter answered:
    Yes, sir, you know that I love You.

Jesus asked:
>Peter, do you love ME?

And he said:
>Yes, sir, I do love YOU.

And Jesus asked for the third time:
>Peter, do you love ME?

And Peter said:
>Please, sir, stop it,
>you know that I love YOU.

And then Jesus said:
>In that case,
>take care of the others,
>take care of all the others.

He got his vision,
the vision of Jesus,
a vision
in which
that Jesus,
that Son of God,
sees the whole of humankind
as hanging,
as belonging together:
>I am the trunk,
>you are the branches.
>He is the Head,
>we are the members.

According to Jesus,
we belong together,
we form one body;
according to Jesus,
there is only one human being,
HUMANITY.
>That is his vision,
>but it is as well his working plan,
>it is his organizational project.

It is not only a vision.
If this is really true,

if we really belong together,
then that little parking-boy*
in the street,
in his rags,
and with his missing background,
belongs to you.
And if he is sick
and hungry
and miserable,
   then we are sick
   and hungry
   and miserable;
     until things are changed,
     until the vision of Jesus
     is translated into reality.
If we are to be one,
and we are to be one
just like Peter and Paul
finally were one,
   then we have to break our bread,
   we have to break our bread.

*Street urchins who "guard" parked cars.

29.

THE FORBIDDEN
EMERGENCY EXIT

Jesus,
Peter,
James,
and John
   climbed a mountain,
   to be by themselves
   and to be with God.
   And suddenly Jesus
   started to change,
   he started to develop,
   he started to shine.
   The fatigue disappeared from his eyes;
   his hands and his feet,
   dirtied by the dusty climb,
   became cleaner and cleaner;
   even his clothes changed;
   they became whiter and whiter,
   they lost all their dirt
   and all the traces
   of their contact with the earth.
      And there Jesus was,
      glorified
      and risen,
      happy
      and fresh,
      young
      and shining,

radiant as the sun,
a new man,
a new creature.
Peter,
James,
and John,
    looking at this
    forgot all the rest;
    the end of their walk
    had come,
    so they thought;
    heaven was on the point of
    opening,
    and indeed heaven
    did open:
    And out of heavens' door
    came Moses,
    and out of the heavenly gate
    came Elijah.
Peter,
James,
and John
    were in heavenly company.
    They must have started to shine too,
    and Peter said:
    This is wonderful,
    it is wonderful for us
    to be here,
    let us stay.
    Let us make tents,
    glory, glory,
    alleluia.
        An escape from this world
        seemed to be open to them;
        they forgot all about the rest,
        they forgot all about the crippled
        and the sick,
        about evil and injustice,

about riots and collapsing towers,
sin and theft.
There
in front of them,
behind Moses and Elijah and Jesus
was an emergency exit
from here to there,
from the earth into heaven.
They wanted to be
    with Jesus,
    with Moses,
    with Elijah,
    with God.
They did not even listen
to what those three were talking about.
They should have listened,
  because those three
  were talking about
  the next phase in Jesus' life,
  about his confrontation in this world
  with the evil in it,
  about his fight with it,
  about his suffering,
  about his death,
  about the new exodus,
      the new pass-over,
      the new struggle,
      the new victory.
The criticism
against religious people
is very often
that they are not bothering,
that they are not caring
about this world.
The criticism is that they leave
the care for this world
to others,
the not so religious,

or the non-religious.
   Peter,
   James,
   and John,
   had to learn their lesson,
   and suddenly
   there was a cloud,
   there was a voice,
   there was an announcement,
   and there was a command:
      This is MY SON,
      listen to him,
   and Moses disappeared,
   and Elijah disappeared,
   the escape was closed,
   the door was shut,
   and they saw only Jesus
   left standing there,
      the fatigue creeping into his eyes,
      his hands and feet dirty again,
      his clothes visibly under the impression
      of his stay here on earth;
      and they went back with him,
      down from the mountain,
      down to the earth
      to continue his fight,
      and he asked us to come with him.

Part IV

SUFFERING AND CROSS

30.

IN SILENT TEARS

Palm-Passion Sunday,
and all the readings are about
   death,
   suffering,
   and about the fact
   that unless
   the wheat of grain
   falls to the ground
   and dies,
   it will be useless.
It has to die,
it has to fall,
it has to go through suffering
and through death.
   We all know this;
   we are all participating
   in suffering and death,
   in pain and loneliness,
   in fear and guilt,
   in tension and anxiety.
Not a son,
but *our* son got lost;
not a daughter,
but *our* daughter disappeared;
not a husband,
but *my* husband drinks;
not a wife,
but *my* wife nags,
day and night;

not a stomach,
but *my* stomach bleeds;
not a past,
but *my* past hurts;
not a future,
but *my* future is uncertain;
   and we protest
   aloud
   and in silent tears.
   And time and time again
   people among us
   rise up,
   and they say:
   We have to change all this,
   we have to change the world,
   we have to change the structures,
   we have to change humanity,
   we have to create a new humanity,
   we have to recreate it,
      we will be like gods,
      you will be like gods,
      here on earth,
      and they forget,
      and we forget,
      who made that suggestion
      first.
It all seems impossible;
we are passing away
on a decaying star.
It seems useless
to kill anybody
in view of that better future
that always seems to be waiting
around the corner,
but that never seems to come
to us over here.
   Whether we like it or not,
   this is the world in which we live,
   this is the life we live.

And the difficulty is
that we cannot even take this situation,
this human condition,
as a reason to sit down,
to fold or to put up our hands,
to surrender,
or to take refuge
in whatever gadget or distraction
we might be able to construct.
We are not allowed
to use the facts
to justify those facts,
   to justify the existence among us
   of injustice
      and loneliness
      and fear
      and sadness
      and guilt
      and anxiety.
   We have to fight against them.
   It is like our house,
   the room in which we live,
   the garden we have,
   the shamba we bought:
      The fact that that house will get dirty again
      is no reason not to clean it;
      the fact that that room will get dusty again
      is no reason not to dust it;
      the fact that that garden will get weedy again
      is no reason not to weed it;
      the fact that that shamba will get dry again,
      is no reason not to water it.
But even then,
why all this,
why this suffering,
why,
why,
why,
why,

why?
It is our greatest
and final why.
    We can talk very nicely,
    theo-logically,
    but can we escape the idea,
    that the agony of his creation
    must
    IN A SENSE
    be laid on the shoulders of God,
    as his responsibility?
    I know
    the idea is
    officially
    blasphemous.
    True,
    but is that not what we tell
    each other
    when facing death
    and sickness and pain
    and suffering?
And to say
that people
and creation
suffer
because of their sins,
is that not begging the question?
    And that is why
    it is good for us to know
    that God came down
    in Jesus Christ
    to suffer like us,
    to suffer with us
    aloud
    and in silent tears,
    during his life
    in prison
    and on the cross.

That is the way
in which he,
so to speak,
vindicated himself
in the suffering eyes
and ears and heads
of all those
who cry
WITH HIM:
My God,
. why did you forsake me?
That is the way
in which
he showed,
through suffering, death, and resurrection,
that all this life
and that all our lives
are indeed a passing phase,
through which
we build ourselves
in God's image
to be with him
to be like him
now
and
after this.

31.

THE CROSS: HORIZONTAL AND VERTICAL

It was late in the evening,
they were sitting at their last supper;
he was there,
and they were there.
They did not know
that this was going to be
their last evening meal.
But he knew,
and he spoke to them.
They had been with him
for two
or for three years,
and yet
he had remained a stranger to them.
They did not understand.
This last supper
was a final proof and demonstration
of their misunderstanding.
He,
Jesus, spoke,
    about what they should do,
    when he would be away,
    about being servants to each other,
    and therefore
    about working great works in this world,
    about taking up their responsibilities,

about not being troubled,
about not being afraid,
about the Spirit he was going to send them
in this world,
to continue his work.
Philip cut him short.
He said:
Lord, show us the Father
and we will be satisfied.
He interrupted Jesus' talk
about his
and their work
in this world.
He said:
Show us the Father,
and forget about the rest.
Give us a shortcut into happiness,
a shortcut from this world to heaven.
It was the temptation
of a pious man,
the temptation to escape from this world,
or,
if that is not possible,
and most times it is not,
then, at least,
to escape from real responsibility:
Show us the Father,
and we will be saved;
that is all we want,
to be fulfilled.
Jesus refused;
he said:
You stay in the world,
do not be afraid,
take up your task,
I will send you the Spirit
to help you.

Did you ever hear about that woman
in France
called Simone Weil?
She was so tired
of all kinds of Christians
who prayed for justice and peace,
while Jews and proletarians were persecuted
and victimized
and who did not Do
anything
to help their prayers to be heard,
that she decided
    to live a life
    without that escape,
    to live as if
    God did not exist.
Did you ever hear about that man
in Germany,
a clergyman, Dietrich Bonhoeffer,
who got so fed up
with all the prayers said by Christians
to be delivered from the dictator Adolf Hitler,
without those Christians
organizing anything against him,
that he, after having organized a coup
and after having been arrested
and condemned to death,
wrote
in his last letter
just before his execution
that we should live as if
God did not exist.
He meant to say
    that we should dare to live
    our responsibilities
    and that we should not ask our Father
    in heaven
    to take over
    leaving all to him.

When confronted with his task,
Philip
only asked for the Father,
and he was wrong.
Some modern people,
fed up with all Christian Philips,
say:
 Let us forget about the Father,
 and they are wrong too.
We should ask for the Father,
we should be with the Father,
but not in a way
that we escape our responsibilities.
Jesus shouted for his Father
while hanging on the cross,
he looked up,
he searched the horizon,
he sought between the stars;
his Father did not come,
but his Father sent him
the power
to stay with us,
to take up his responsibility among us,
even on the cross,
that was his cross.
He looked up vertically,
but he stayed with us
horizontally.
That is what our position should be:
 To look up for the Father,
 vertically,
 but not only that;
 that is not all,
 that was the mistake of Philip.
We should look up
to get the force and the power
to work around us
in this world,
in this country,

horizontally,
   to help
   to create
   justice
   and peace,
   dignity
   and universality.
Let us be like Jesus,
please,
let us be like Jesus,
and let us not use the Father
as an excuse
to feel glorified already,
so glorified
that we forget
and forsake
our task.

32.

FOR OPPRESSORS
AND OPPRESSED

Once upon a time,
there was that blind man
who was healed by him.
Three times the scholars of Israel
came to him
to convince him
that Jesus,
who had healed him from his blindness,
was a sinner.
   They did not succeed;
   the man saw,
   he remained seeing,
   he did not want to be that blind again.
But finally they did succeed,
because only a very short time afterwards
that same Jesus
was hanging on the cross,
not between two candles,
or between flowers
like in a church,
but between two thieves,
two murderers.
   He was hanging on that cross,
   because they had made him a sinner.
   The temple leaders said
      that he interrupted the services;
   the synagogue leaders said

that he blasphemed;
the pharisees said
    that he did not keep the law;
the people said
    that he upset the existing order;
and the Romans said
    that he was a subversive freedom fighter.
He died as a sinner, because
    the religious leaders,
    the political leaders,
    and society
    had made him a sinner.
He was the victim of oppression,
from the side of the church,
from the side of the state,
from the side of the nation.
    In some places,
    on this, our planet,
    this is understood very well.
    In those places,
    his cross
    and his way of the cross
    are the center
    of the popular religious year.
In South America
the poor workers on the plantations,
perhaps the most lost and forsaken group
of people in our world of today,
do not so much celebrate
Jesus' triumph,
his victory,
or his resurrection.
They do not recognize him
in that victorious state.
It is not their state.
They recognize him
    as a fellow,
    as an equal,

as a comrade,
as a friend,
as a colleague,
in his suffering
and
on his cross.
They are able to identify with him,
when he is standing
before the priests,
before the police,
before the magistrates,
and
before the oppressive town mob.
It is at those moments
that they are like him,
that they are really like him,
and he like them,
really like them.
    The dominant church
and its leaders
try to convince those people,
"the wretched of the earth,"
that Jesus was dying on the cross
because of their poor,
                private,
                and personal sins,
because of their poor lust
and greed.
But THEY know better,
THEY know much better:
    He died
    because of the sins
    of those leaders.
    He died
    because of the oppressive
    religious,
    political,
    and social structures.

Jesus is with them,
with the poor,
with the wretched;
he is of their flesh,
he is of their blood,
he is of their class.
   He put his divinity
   in a wardrobe
   between heavenly mothballs
   to be with them,
   to be like them.
In North America
the African slaves
had
that very same outlook
in those matters:
   Were you there when they crucified my Lord,
   were you there?
And the answer is:
YES,
we,
the black slaves
were there
in his agony,
on his cross.
   Such an attitude
   can,
   of course,
   be abused
   by the masters.
   It was abused
   by them.
   They told their slaves,
   or their lackeys from their churches
   told those slaves:
      Be glad
      and rejoice

that you have a real cross
to bear,
alleluia,
like Jesus,
alleluia.
In the end
you will be better off
than those,
who are now better off
than you,
alleluia,
amen.
That is why Karl Marx said
that religion
but especially Christianity
is
"the groaning of the oppressed,"
a sedative,
a sleeping pill,
dawa* against the nerves,
opium,
a cup full of alcohol.
But that is not so.
He did not get the full picture.
To the poor,
Jesus
is more than just that.
    Those slaves knew
    that Jesus,
    showing himself as a slave,
    was not showing himself
    as he really is:
        GOD ALMIGHTY.
    Just as they,
    like slaves,
    were not

*Medicine.

the real ones
they are:
    MIGHTY FREE PEOPLE.
In their knowledge
of Jesus
and his misery,
in their knowledge
of themselves
and their misery,
there is that corrective,
and therefore
that redeeming element.
    Jesus was rejected by people,
    but he was as well rejected by God.
    In the bitter,
    in that very bitter end,
    he shouted aloud:
    Father,
    for heaven's sake,
    where are you?
It is at this point
that the mystery
deepens still more.
Sin
gets still more absurd.
Jesus identified
with those who are rejected by people;
he identified as well
with those
that are accepted by people,
but rejected by God.
    He identified
    with the oppressed,
    but he identified as well
    with the oppressors
    who are rejected by God
    because they trample and abuse

the poor and the lowly,
the widow and the orphan,
the slaves and the servants.
He identified
with the dehumanized,
but as well with the inhuman dehumanizers;
he identified
with the dying victim,
but he did not forget the
victimizer.
    He died for the prisoner
    and for his warden;
    for the tortured one
    and for his torturer.
    He wanted to bring the oppressed
    into glory,
    but he wanted as well
    to break the oppressor open
    to his real
    human dignity.
He wanted to make both groups
correspond to God's idea of them.
    He said
    that
    to save
    the rich
    would be
    more difficult
    than
    to save
    the poor.
He wanted,
however,
to save
both groups.
He wanted
to save them all.

He tried to be the bridge
between the two,
a bridge
over troubled
and bitter
water.
His anguish,
the anguish
of our redeemer,
must have been
terrible,
and his cross
immense.
He experienced in his own body,
in his own psychology,
the powers
that tear humankind
apart.
He died
of utter exhaustion,
rejected by others,
rejected by God,
AND HE WAS DEAD,
REALLY DEAD
FOR THREE DAYS.
He died for you,
he died for me.
Why did he die for you,
why did he die for me?
Do you belong to the oppressed,
or do you belong to the oppressors?
Do I belong to the oppressed,
or do I belong to the oppressors?
Why did he die for you,
why did he die for me?
I am afraid
that every one
of us

reading this text
belongs to both groups.
   We are oppressed,
   and we are oppressors
   if only
   because we profit from a system
   in which we can whistle
   for a prostitute,
   and refuse to help
   a starving man,
   going our way,
   going our own way.
      HE DIED FOR US.
      HE DIED FOR YOU.
      HE DIED FOR ME.

Part V

RESURRECTION
AND
ASCENSION

33

IT REALLY STARTED
AT EASTER

Easter.
Jesus rose.
He returned.
The tomb was empty,
    and slowly,
    slowly,
    his disciples started to understand
    what had happened.
    Their first reactions were far from encouraging:
    They were frightened
    out of their wits;
    within that exclusive male circle
    the first reports
    were qualified as
    women's talk;
    they did not recognize him,
    they could not believe it;
but then slowly
their belief started to grow,
not so much,
I think,
because of what they saw
outside themselves,
or because they touched him,
but much more
because they felt his power in them:
    an urge to go out,

an urge, again, to leave things behind,
an urge to take risks,
an urge to change, again, their life:
He did not only come back;
he came back with power
in them.
In fact
all that coming-back talk
is a bit tricky.
It is at the resurrection
that Jesus really comes
into this world,
into his power,
his divine power.
The rest of his life,
the life before,
should only be seen
and was only seen
by the apostles and the evangelists
in the light of this real coming:
risen,
in power and majesty.
There is that fantastic scene
in the beginning of the fifth chapter
of the book of Revelation.
There is a very large hall,
full of angels and other creatures;
in the back of the hall
is a throne
and on that throne
God.
People in the hall
are not looking at him;
they are looking at his right hand.
In that hand God holds a book,
a closed book,
a book with seven seals,
the book that contains

all the chapters
of the history of this world,
of human history.
The plan,
his plan.
An angel steps forward
from behind God,
and that angel asks:
    Who is prepared to open the book?
    Who is allowed?
There is a great silence,
a very audible hush.
There is nobody in heaven
or on earth
allowed to open the book.
The silence continues,
until an old man
almost whispers:
    Yes,
    there is one.
And at that moment
a lamb
enters the hall.
And that does not mean that a lamb
with four legs
and a tail
entered;
it means that a person
who had functioned on earth
as a lamb,
a sacrificial lamb,
entered.
He went forward,
and he received the book
in power and majesty,
and the whole heavens
suddenly burst out
in praise and song,

in cheering and hosannah,
in alleluia and amen.
    And it is then
    that his real role starts;
    it is at that moment
    that he really entered
    into his possession,
    that he really came to do
    the will of the father,
    from whom he had received the book,
        in this world,
        or perhaps better
        not in this world,
        but in that other world
        we believe in:
           another world,
           a better world,
           a kinder world,
           a milder world
           a more divine world.
The difference between us
and all the others
who believe in the possibility
of that better world
is not that belief;
    it is the belief
    that this world is judged;
    and that does not mean
    that it is condemned;
    it means that this world
    is seen as subordinate,
    as subject,
        to another world,
        that world
        from which the book
        and the opener of the book
        are coming.
        Alleluia.

34.

HE MADE HIMSELF VISIBLE

I think
that celebrating Easter
we very often are
too superficial,
when celebrating and analyzing that feast.
   Jesus was away;
   he died,
   he had been killed,
   he had been betrayed,
   he had disappeared from among the living;
   all contact had been broken,
   not so much by him,
   but much more by them,
   who had left him on the cross;
   there was no signal any more,
   no communication.
And THEN he appears:
first to Mary Magdalen.
She does not recognize him;
she thinks he is a gardener,
a shamba boy.*
   She asks him:
   "Where is he?"
   "Where did you put him?"
   And he said:

*Field hand.

"Mary."
And she said:
"Rabboni,"
just as two persons
after an interruption
over the phone,
after a breakdown
caused by one or another
disaster,
say:
"Hello,
hello."
And then he appears to the eleven,
and to show that he is the real one,
that he is the old one,
he takes from their table
a piece of grilled fish,
fish and chips,
and he eats it,
he swallows it,
he starts to digest it:
He is back,
he is really back,
alleluia, alleluia, alleluia,
but so what?
I think we must go further
and deeper
to understand the dramatic events
of those days.
We should use our human experience,
our human expertise,
and our psychological insight
much more.
First there were the stories
about the empty tomb.
Everybody is, of course,
excited about them:
the disciples,

the high priests,
and the soldiers
from the Roman military police.
Nobody is said to have been glad
about those empty tomb stories.
In fact it is said
that they all were afraid,
frightened stiff;
    the soldiers were afraid
    because he had escaped them,
    and they had no idea how;
    the high priests were so unhappy about it
    that they paid money to those soldiers
    to spread the story
    that he had been stolen by his disciples;
    and those disciples of his were not glad
    because they too were afraid;
    we should not forget,
    that after all,
    they all had betrayed him
    rather badly.
Everybody had a good reason
to be afraid of that man
Jesus.
That Jesus
they had treated so badly,
and who now
was no longer in his tomb
in which they had sealed him so carefully,
suffocated in pounds and pounds,
a hundred pounds according to the most exact estimate,
of perfumes, oils, and preservatives.
    Those disciples knew about their Bible,
    they knew about other empty tombs,
    about Elijah,
    who had been taken up,
    about Enoch,
    who had been taken up,

about Moses,
whose tomb never had been found.
An empty tomb
meant to be taken up,
to be taken up
by God.
    No wonder that Peter,
    the man who betrayed him so badly,
    had something to think about
    when he went home,
    after having convinced himself
    of the emptiness of the tomb.
Everybody was amazed,
but everybody was afraid as well:
    Had they not betrayed him,
    had they not given up hope,
    had they not left him in the cold,
    had they not underestimated him?
What was he going to do,
what was he going to do,
what was he going to do?
    He who had said:
    If a village does not receive you,
    leave it,
    and blow its dust from your shoes.
    He who had said:
    It would have been better for this traitor
    never to have been born.
    He who told the story
    of the man
    who had not been properly dressed
    and who was cast out in the fire,
    an eternal fire,
    gnashing his teeth
    day and night.
What was he going to do?
What was he going to do?
What was he going to do?

And then he started to appear to them,
to visit them,
to speak to them,
to be friendly with them,
to eat fish with them,
and it is only then,
only then,
that it is reported
that they could not believe their eyes.
And I think that this does not mean
that they could not believe that he had risen;
that they believed already;
the belief in a resurrection
and in the fact
that God can raise the dead to life
was a rather common belief
in their time.
I think
that they could not believe their eyes
because he came to them
and because he was friendly,
as if nothing had happened,
as if they had not betrayed him;
he seemed to have forgotten completely.
He only said:
    Peace,
    and
    Do not be afraid,
    and
    in all appearances to the group of them
    there is that mention
    of forgiveness.
He came
and he forgave.
And they are said
to have been with a joy
so great
that they could not believe it.

Do you see it?
Do you see it?
The resurrection was terrific.
But when they heard about it
they were frightened rigid.
What was he going to do?
He came
and he forgave.
    They were saved,
    they were reassured,
    they were rescued,
    they would live on.
But he did not allow them
to live on
just like that.
    Their salvation
    was not going to remain as empty as his tomb;
    their salvation had to be filled up:
        They had to repent,
        they had to turn to God,
        they had to build a human community,
        they had to love each other,
        they had to go out and preach,
        not only the resurrection,
        not even so much perhaps that resurrection,
        but the forgiveness of sins;
        they had to go out,
        to realize in this world,
        the message he had brought them
        from that other world
        he came from:
            PEACE,
            a peace that can
            now
            be based on justice
            and on justice
            in the future,
            a peace

that can be built only
on forgiving the past.
A peace that is a personal concern,
a justice that is a personal concern;
but a peace that is as well a common concern
and a justice that is as well a common concern,
because they are the rock
on which God's kingdom
will be built.

35.

THE THOMAS TEST

You know the story,
how the disciples,
after his death and resurruction
sat together,
and suddenly, he,
Jesus,
appeared in the midst of them.
They were amazed,
they could not believe their eyes.
And to prove that they might
they gave him a piece of fish,
a normal piece of freshly fried fish,
    and he took it,
    he put it in his mouth,
    he chewed,
    he swallowed;
    they looked very carefully;
    the fish disappeared;
    it did not fall through,
    it was taken up.
    He was real,
    he was no ghost,
    no spirit or evil dream.
They were satisfied
and believed their eyes.
    Thomas came late;
    they informed him
    enthusiastically.
    He did not believe.

He must have thought
that the others had dreamt,
that the desire to see him
had made them
see him,
    as a hungry man
    dreams of bread,
    as a man in the desert
    sees the water
    he is longing for
    in his thirst.
They told him about the fish,
but he laughed at their fish.
He disqualified their test.
He put his own norms,
another test,
a more realistic experiment.
He said:
    Let him show me his hands,
    let him show me his feet,
    let him show me his side,
    let him show me his wounds,
    and if he has the wounds,
    I will believe,
    but if there are no wounds
    and no scars,
    then
    forget about him,
    forget about your fish.
A week later,
he appeared again.
Thomas was with them:
    Was he an imposter,
    was he a tramp,
    a conjuring trick,
    a projection,
    a ghost,
    or a spirit?

The others looked at Thomas.
He rose and approached the appearance,
and he said:

> Please, sir, may I see your hands?
> Please, sir, may I see your feet?
> Please, sir, may I see your side?

> And he saw the hands,
> and he saw the feet,
> and he saw the side,
> and he saw the wounds,
> and he saw the scars,
> and he believed,
> leaving us a test,
> the THOMAS TEST.

A test you measure
your Christianity with.
If you are a Christian,
a follower of Jesus Christ,

> then:

> Please, sir, may I see your hands?
> Please, sir, may I see your feet?
> Please, sir, may I see your side?

And if you have wounds and scars,
like he had wounds and scars,

> because of your interest
> and thirst
> for justice
> and honesty
> and integrity
> and everything he died and lived for,
> I will believe.

Then,
but only then,
you will have passed the test:
the THOMAS TEST.

36.

BREAKING THROUGH
THE CIRCLE

Thomas was absent that evening.
He had been absent at a very critical evening,
the evening that Jesus
gave his disciples their mission
and the power to forgive.
  Thomas had been absent
  while all the others were praying
  and hoping
  and believing.
From the story,
as it came to us,
we might even conclude
why Thomas was absent.
He was absent,
because he did not believe any more;
he was absent,
because he did not hope any more;
he was absent,
because he did not pray any more.
And even the reason for all that
negativity
in his attitude
is mentioned too.
  Thomas had,
  together with the others,
  SEEN the mighty deeds of Jesus,
  his healings,
  his exorcisms,

his walking over the waters,
his breaking of the bread.
Thomas had,
together with the others,
HEARD the voice of God,
when heaven tore apart above Jesus.
    Thomas had,
    together with the others,
    SMELLED the good wine at Cana
    and the enormous catches of fish
    in Galilee.
Thomas had,
together with the others,
TASTED that fresh bread,
somewhere in a field,
when HE broke and broke and broke.
    Thomas had TOUCHED,
    together with the others,
    time and time again,
    the Jesus
    whom he loved.
And just like
all the others,
he had
    SEEN,
    HEARD,
    SMELLED,
    TASTED,
    and TOUCHED not only that,
        but behind
        and beyond
        and through
        all that:
            GOD
            and many realities DIVINE.
But disappointed
by the suffering on the cross,
he had narrowed his vision,

he had restricted his world,
and he said:
    From now on,
    I am going to believe
    only what I see
        and hear
        and taste
        and smell
        and touch
        and nothing more,
    like so many around us,
    and perhaps even among us,
    are doing,
    in the name of emancipation,
    in the name of development,
    in the name of civilization.
    People who lived
    up to some years ago
    in a world
    of spirits,
    ancestors,
    and God,
    in a world hidden
    behind and beyond and through
    all around us,
    narrowed their vision,
    shortened their view
    to a world,
    so small,
    that Coca-Cola and Fanta
    and other tangibles
    are not only important
    but the real thing,
        the world of food,
        the world of drink,
        the world of a mate,
        and endless, meaningless
        social chatter.

The world of Thomas,
the world of the man
who was away,
while the others
    believed,
    prayed,
    and hoped.
But then
there was that other evening
that Jesus came,
and that Thomas
was together with the others,
and he saw,
and he smelled,
and he touched,
and he tasted,
and he heard,
        and he said,
        he could not avoid
        but saying:
        MY LORD
        AND
        MY GOD.
        And by saying that
        he broke
        through the circle,
        through the limits,
        through the borders
        that he had drawn
        around himself:
    MY LORD
    AND
    MY GOD.
        He saw,
        beyond,
        behind;
        he saw
        through.

37.

EXPATRIATE JESUS

Many "old boys,"
from very devout Christian schools,
remain brave followers of Jesus Christ.
Others, however,
are very outspoken
in their refusal of that same Jesus of Nazareth.
    Their reasons are often the same.
    They say and write things like:
    Jesus is a stranger in Africa,
    he is an expatriate,
    he is from another world,
    he is a product from the West,
    he is an imperialist,
    he is a colonialist,
    he is pretentious.
You cannot be faithful to African culture
and obey him;
you cannot be yourself as an African
and be a Christian.
He is an alienator.
    In Emmaus,
    to the northeast of Africa,
    Jesus appeared to two friends.
    They did not recognize him.
    To them he was a stranger.
    He did not even seem to have heard
    about what recently happened in Jerusalem.
    A stranger in Jerusalem.
    A stranger in Emmaus.

Emmaus is not the only time
that Jesus played that role,
or may we say that game,
of being a stranger.
    John the Baptist said:
    There is a stranger among you.
    He meant Jesus.
    Nathanael said:
    What good can that stranger be,
    from that sub-, sub-, sub-location
    Nazareth?
    He meant Jesus.
    The woman from Samaria met him
    as a stranger.
    Nicodemus waited until it was dark
    to meet that strange and foreign
    teacher.
Our friends from Emmaus thought
that they were walking
with a stranger.
    And HE,
    HE
    did NOT reveal HIMSELF to them.
    HE,
    HE waited
    until THEY
    recognized him.
    It had to come
    from WITHIN THEM.
It is very true to say
that Jesus is a stranger
to many,
maybe even to all of us.
    He is a Jew,
    he is an Asian,
    from Asia Minor,
    but nevertheless from Asia.

He lived two thousand years ago
in a completely different situation,
in a completely different environment.
He really is a stranger.
But,
if you believe in him,
then it must have been You
who recognized something in Him.
And if this recognition comes from you,
how could he
at the same time
be strange to you?
That is what happened to the two friends
from Emmaus.
Jesus did not reveal himself,
he did not tell who he was.
He took bread.
He broke it,
and They recognized him,
Him,
the bread-breaker,
the universal
Companion.

38.

THEY LOST THEIR HEAD

While the disciples looked up,
they lost their head,
and their heads too.
He became smaller and smaller.
A cloud intervened,
and off
he was.
    God had been with them
    in Jesus.
    They had become intimate.
    He had taught them,
    fed them,
    paid their taxes;
    he had fried fish for them,
    he even had washed their feet.
    He had promised them
    a new earth,
    a new heaven,
    a kingdom to come,
    and off he was.
        It was as if all the doors
        of heaven,
        that had been opened
        for about thirty-three years,
        closed again.
        Curtains were drawn.
        Shutters rattled down.
        Lights went out.
        A foggy cloud appeared:
        It took all vision away.

They lost their head,
and losing their head,
they lost their heads too.
   They were dazzled,
    they remained looking.
   They were paralyzed,
    petrified on the spot.
Two angels had to appear
to get them on the move.
They stumbled down the mountain,
they found their way to Jerusalem.
They,
   the beginning of the church,
   the beginning of Christ's body,
they with their worldwide mission
   locked themselves up
   in an upper room:
   Upper rooms are always safer
   than ground-floor ones;
   and they did not know
   what to do:
They had lost their head,
their head was in the clouds.
   You know how a man
   with his head in the clouds
   reacts:
      He sits down on chairs
      that are not there
      and he hurts himself;
      he waits for buses
      that do not arrive;
      he makes a sandwich
      and eats his paper napkin;
      he wets a stamp
      to put it on his letter
      and sticks it on the table.
   A man with his head
   in the clouds
   is useless,

hopeless;
his body stumbles along,
    falls,
        gets lost.
Those disciples,
the church
with its head in the clouds
at the right hand of the Father,
did not know what to do:
    There were no signals,
    there was no communication,
    and they sat down
    and waited
    behind locked doors
    until,
    until
    the signals suddenly came through again,
    the contact was restored,
    even to the extent
    that there were sparkles
    everywhere:
        light,
        fire,
        noise,
        breath,
        wind,
        storm,
        enthusiasm,
        and SPIRIT,
        his Spirit.
            And they rose,
            and they entered
            into the life
            of this world.

Part VI

PENTECOST
AND
FOLLOW-UP

39.

THE SPIRIT GOT YOU

There is the story
about that old man
in the wilderness,
sitting under a bush,
wishing he was dead.
His name: Elijah.
   He said:
   I am no better than my ancestors,
   and he lay down,
   closed his eyes,
   and fell asleep,
   hoping never to wake up
   any more.
But an angel came;
the angel touched him,
the angel kicked him,
and the angel said:
   Get up and eat.
   And he saw in front of him
   water and bread;
   he drank the water,
   and he ate the bread
and he lay down again,
closed his eyes,
and fell asleep,
hoping never to wake up
anymore.
The angel returned,
and the angel touched him,

the angel kicked him,
and the angel said:
 Get up and eat,
 or the journey will be too long for you.
 He got up,
 and he ate,
 and he drank,
 and he walked,
 all the way
 to the mountain of the Lord.
Who is Elijah?
It is you.
Who is Elijah?
It is me.
 It is you and it is me
 at the moment
 that we too
  sit down,
 that we too
  lay down
  and say:
  I am no better than all
  the good-for-nothings
  before me.
  I am going to give up,
  I am going to close my eyes,
  I am going to fall asleep;
  let others go on,
  let them take over.
Brothers, sisters,
did you never try
to sit under that tree?
Did you never try
to give up?
Did the world never seem too much for you,
and did the safari in this world
never seem too long?
Were you never like Elijah?

I think you were,
I think I was.
But I too was kicked by an angel,
and you too
must have been kicked by an angel,
otherwise you would not have been
over here
this morning.
Philosophers tell us
that God is a metaphysical reality,
that God is beyond our scope;
positivists and scientists
tell us
that God is an unverifiable idea.
   Do you believe that?
   Do you really believe that?
   I do not.
God only a metaphysical reality?
God only an unverifiable idea?
How can those people say so?
Did they never feel God gripping their guts?
Did you never feel him
   in your stomach,
   in your head,
   in your kidneys?
   I bet you did.
Saint Paul says
   that we did feel him,
   that you did feel him,
   that I feel him,
   because he says
      that the Holy Spirit
      marked us with his seal,
      that he burnt his mark in us
      in fire and smoke
      in pain and stench.
      The Holy Spirit got us, he caught you,
      you drowned in the Holy Spirit.

The Holy Spirit is like water;
the Bible says again and again
that the Holy Spirit is like water.
He is given in water,
he is given with water.
Elijah drank that water
and he pulled through.
    You are filled with that water,
    and he is going to pull you through as well.
    He is never going to let you go,
    he is never going to let you escape:
        You are marked,
        we are marked,
        we are signed
        forever and ever.
The Holy Spirit is like water;
water is powerful, man,
water is powerful.
Look at the floor of this chapel;
do you see the cracks,
do you see them?
    The builder of this chapel
    saw them too,
    and he wondered why the floor cracked.
    He thinks he found out:
    There is water under the floor,
    he says,
    and that powerful water is pushing up
    that heavy stone floor.
Water is powerful,
water gives life;
it falls over a dried-up field,
it disappears in the field,
it seems to be away,
you do not see it any more,
    but then everything
    in that field
    starts to get green,

to get flowers,
to get seeds;
everything starts to live.
Elijah was fed up,
and the Spirit got him up.
That Spirit is going to get you up too:
the Spirit in us,
he feeds us,
he pushes us,
he helps us,
he does wonderful things.
He makes us do wonderful things,
he makes us speak languages
we do not know.
Did you never speak a language
you did not know
under the influence of that Spirit?
Oh, yes, you did!
Do you remember,
you had to meet somebody,
you did not like him,
you made up your mind to tell him that,
to be rude,
to tell him the truth.
And there he came.
You opened your mouth
to be rude,
to tell him the truth,
but the words that came out
were kind
and polite;
the Spirit got you again.
He did it again;
let him do it
again
and again.

40.

THE FAITH THAT SAVES

Somewhere in his letter
Saint James writes:
   Take the case, brothers and sisters,
   of someone who has never done a single good act,
   but who claims that he has faith,
   a faith that saves him.
An invitation to take a case.
Let us take such a case,
or even some of them.
   One night
   in a hospital over here
   in this country,
   there was a meeting,
   a charismatic meeting;
   you know them,
   alleluia,
   alleluia,
   Spirit come,
   and the Spirit did come.
     A nurse,
     whose name I am not going to mention,
     went to that meeting,
     although there was a patient,
     who really needed her that evening.
     Will that faith save her?
In a mission
there are two priests.
One is very pious;
his breviary is yellow,

220

in shreds,
the pages are worn away;
his rosary is said so often,
that the beads start to fall through the thread.
He is in church always
   in the morning,
   in the evening,
   and in between,
but people are waiting in front of his office,
and in front of his confessional box,
and the man at the door repeats all the time:
Father did not yet finish his devotions,
Father did not yet finish his prayers,
you will have to wait,
and you too,
and you as well.
And even when the father comes out of his prayer,
he is so rough
and so cool
and so ununderstanding
that even the dogs in that mission
run away
when they see him coming,
and the children all turn their faces another way
when they see him come,
and they do not run away
only because their mothers hold their hands.
Is the faith/of that father going to save him?
   And then there is the other one;
   he does not pray so very much;
   he lost his breviary some time ago,
    and he only fingers his rosary now and then,
   when he cannot sleep during the night;
   he prays,
   but definitely not as much as the first one;
   but he is always helpful,
   he helps the really hungry,
   he helps the really naked,

he is efficient,
people do not have to wait
for ages
in front of his office;
he is kind
and happy
and reliable;
he visits the sick
and the poor
and even the prisoners from his parish,
and everybody likes him,
and everybody greets him,
and the children would all run
to touch him,
if their mothers would not hold their hands.
Is the faith of that father going to save him?
I went with a visitor,
there are always a lot of visitors over here in Nairobi,
to a charismatic church meeting in Pumwami.
The visitor liked it very much;
in Europe and America
those meetings are very new;
sisters go there because it is new,
and sisters like new things;
fathers go there,
because they want to see how to speak about them
to those sisters.
Very many people go there,
but those people in Europe and America
do not know
that over here in Africa,
in Nairobi,
those meetings are nothing extraordinary.
An old man,
an elder with beautiful eyes,
started it off;
he invited the Holy Spirit to come down on them;
they sang a very inviting type of hymn;

then he read a part from the Bible,
then they started to pray,
and they prayed more and more,
and they sang alleluia
at least a hundred times,
and they started to dance,
first rather slowly,
and then quicker and quicker,
they started to jump straight up,
higher and higher,
and people started to speak very strange languages,
and one man said that his headache was suddenly gone,
and another man was converted,
and it was very impressive,
although we did not stay to the end,
and when we walked home,
my visitor said:
    It is very nice,
    but how does it work out,
    are they doing good works?
And he asked that very same question
Saint James asked:
    All that faith is very nice,
    all that talk about being saved
    is very good,
    but if that faith
    is without works,
    then it is dead.
Sometimes we meet people
who seem to have that type of faith.
They are enraptured in the Spirit,
they are drunk in the Spirit
but for the rest nothing seems to happen.
Saint James teaches us
how to think about those people,
how to talk to them.
This is what he suggests telling them:
    You say you have faith,

and I have good deeds;
I will prove to you
that I have faith
by showing you my good deeds;
now you prove to me
that you have faith,
without any good deeds to show.
That is what James said.
I did not invent it.
You can read it for yourself.
  That is how we should live;
  we should have faith,
  but we should have the good works too.
  We should be charismatic,
  but that means
  that as nurses
  you really should be nursing:
  helping, healing, laying hands on,
  holding moist hands,
  cooling sweating heads,
  whispering encouraging words in failing ears,
  carrying away waste,
  putting on fresh dressings,
  listening to the bells,
  being kind and efficient.
  Faith is not only feeling fine
  and saying I am saved;
  it is giving the right medicine
  at the right time;
  it is waking people up
  when they should be waked up;
  it means going to them
  when they are afraid
  and anxious to see you,
  although you might be thinking
  that that patient is
  exaggerating and over-anxious.

We should have the Spirit.
We should like the Spirit.
We have to pray for the Spirit,
 but James adds:
  Have him in an effective way;
  let him lead you to deeds,
  deeds that will save you,
  because they are saving others.

41.

BEING TAKEN UP
IN THE MILL

Job complained:
  My work in this world
  is forced labor,
  my time hired drudgery;
  I am a slave in the sun,
  an alienated worker,
  my nights full of grief,
  in the dark I ask:
    When will it be light?
  In the light I ask:
    When will it be dark?
  There is no hope,
  there is no joy,
  nothing is happening.
Saint Paul complained:
  I am a preacher
  doing my duty,
  I am not going to be paid,
  I did not choose myself
  this responsibility;
  it was forced upon me,
  my reward:
  nothing.
  My service:
  free.
  I am a slave.

And Jesus himself
complained
of being taken up in a mill.
 He went to the house of Simon and Andrew;
 he was hurried to the mother-in-law of Peter;
 she had a fever;
 he went to her,
 he took her hand,
 and helped her up again;
 she went to the kitchen
 and made tea for them.
But then they started to come from all sides,
and he healed them.
But why?
All those people
healed by Jesus
would get sick again.
Even the ones
he raised from the dead
would one day
fall down again,
 and that is maybe the reason
 that he, knowing all this,
 left them very early
 in the morning
 to escape them.
 But his disciples came after him,
 looking for him,
 and they said:
 Come,
 everybody is looking for you.
But he said:
 Let us go away,
 now,
 I have to preach,
 and he went away
 to preach
 and to cast out devils.

But he told those devils
to keep their mouths shut,
not to reveal his power and might,
his name,
and his descent into this world.
All this seems very strange.
He seems to hide.
He seems to run away from his work.
He seems to give up.
Yet it all fits in
with the message
that Saint Mark,
who stressed this point so very much,
wished to give to the followers of Jesus.
It is a message to those who are tired
and discouraged in this world.
    And because it is a message
    to those who are tired
    and discouraged,
    it seems as well
    very often
    a message to us.
        Is it not true,
        that we over here in this town,
            over here in this country,
            over here in this world,
            over here at this university,
        very often ask ourselves
        the questions Job asked
        himself,
        the questions Paul asked
        himself:
            What is it all about?
            There seems to be no progress,
            there seems to be no hope;
            the power of Jesus
            seems to turn sour
            all the time;
            the salvation

Christians talk about
seems to make no difference at all,
and definitely not so very much
difference.
My conversion seems to have lost its gist,
and so on.
Tired,
discouraged,
fed up.
    In Saint Mark's gospel
Jesus suffers in this world
like Job.
Some even call the gospel of Saint Mark
nothing but
"a rather long introduction to the passion story."
In the gospel of Saint Mark
Jesus seems to want to hide his power;
that is why the devils were ordered
to keep quiet.
Jesus wanted only three things:
    He wanted to suffer with us,
    he wanted to preach to us,
    and he wanted to inform us
    that he was going to come back
    in glory.
The preaching of Jesus,
according to Saint Mark,
consisted in the fact
that this world
came to an end when he died
on the cross,
and rose from the dead.
According to Saint Mark
he wanted to make it clear to us
that all we have to do now
is to wait for his return
in glory.
    Mark even seems to suggest
    that in our times,

in the days in which we live,
Jesus is absent from this world,
and that we received the Spirit
to come through this desolate period.
    And it is from that point of view
    that Mark has a message
    in our desolation,
    in our discouragement,
    in our disillusionment.
    When we ask ourselves,
    like Job,
    and in a way
    like Paul:
        Are we really saved,
        did he really come?
    Mark's answer is:
        Yes,
        but not yet fully;
        wait till he comes!
Mark's message is incomplete,
it needs the complementation
given by the other gospels,
just like those other gospels
need the complementation from Mark.
Mark overlooks
the presence of Jesus' power
in this world
now,
a power described
by Saint Paul and by Saint John
and others.
But Mark wrote for those of us,
who feel sick
and tired;
he wrote for the brokenhearted,
and he says:
    Wait
    and see;
    he will come.

42.

ARE YOU A SAVIOR?

A savior to the world,
a new light went up,
God showed his love to the world:
   God, love,
   world, light,
   peace, savior,
   all people.
I very often become very impatient
when I try to listen
to all that type
of religious talk,
during daily radio services,
during "lift up your heart" programs,
and during epilogues.
   I hope that you are not scandalized,
   but I do not believe
   that Jesus is
      a savior
      or a light
      or a power
      or a liberator
      or even useful
      in that most general
      of general ways,
      in that,

what specialists would call,
a-historical
or abstract way.
It does not help,
it really does not help.
I believe that Jesus
is a savior
in another way.
   I believe that Jesus was a savior
   to that marrying couple in Cana
   that ran out of beer,
   and he provided through water,
   through water in their kitchen,
   for the necessary extra cases.
I believe that Jesus was a savior
to that mother in Naim,
who was walking behind
the coffin of her son,
when he told them to open that coffin,
and to do it quickly.
I believe that Jesus was a savior
when he returned to her
that beautiful son,
with his broad chest
and his beautiful hair.
   I believe that he was a savior
   to that father of that mad child
   who had fits
   three times, six times, nine times, twelve times a day,
   and he healed that child,
   and the child suddenly said
   without any fit,
   and without any foam on his lips:
      Thank you, sir,
      thank you,
   because he was normal like you
   and me;
   his fits were over.

I believe that he was a savior to the blind
he met;
to the deaf
he healed;
to the lame
he made jump with joy;
and to the hungry and the thirsty
he fed.

   I believe that he was a savior
   to that miserable miser
   Zaccheus,
   who thought only of money
   and interest
   and capital growth
   of land
   and of farms
   and of cows
   and whose heart HE opened
   to help others.

      I believe that he was a savior
      to that adulterous woman,
      whom he told:
      Okay, your sins are forgiven,
      the past is the past,
      no nonsense anymore,
      think of your family,
      and who went away
      free and saved.

I believe that he was a savior
to that coward called Peter,
whom he promised his prayers
and he added:
   You are going to be hopeless,
   you are going to betray,
   but you never will get lost,
   because I prayed for you.

I believe that he was a savior
to that murderer,

that armed robber,
who was hanging next to him
on a cross
and to whom he said:
    Do not bother,
    take it easy,
    you will be with me
    in a minute or two
    forever
    and ever.
I believe that he was a savior
and that he is a savior,
or should we say nowadays
a liberator,
because he helped,
because he saved,
really,
actually
    those men and women,
    those boys and girls.
And I believe
that he is my savior
because he showed me
while doing all this
how I should live,
and more important still,
how I am able to live
with his help.
    Those who believe in him,
    and in his power,
    are not the ones
    who only murmur:
        Utuhurumie,*
        I am a wretched sinner,
        utuhurumie,
        utuhurumie,
        while beating their chests.

*"Have mercy on us."

Those who believe in him
are not the ones
who only sing:
  Alleluia,
  raising their voices
  and slamming their organs and drums.
Those who believe in him
are not the ones
who only multiply their
  nasadikis*
  in very orthodox ways
  checking their catechism
  or
  the latest World Council of Churches
  or papal statements.
Those who believe in him
are those who try
  to live his type of life.
He lived as a savior,
and they,
the believers,
they too try to live
as saviors,
with his help,
with his spirit,
or, if you prefer that other word,
with his grace.
Are you a believer?
Do you try to live as a savior
to the people around you?
Are you a follower of Christ?
  You father,
  while educating your sons and daughters;
  you mother,
  while running your family;
  you, mwalimu,†

*Credos.

†Teacher.

while teaching the hundreds
and in the long run
even the thousands of children
entrusted to you;
you, administrator,
with all the powers of your papers
and their clips,
your pencils, files, and drawers;
you, policeman,
with your stick and your statements
and your dog;
you politician,
with your responsibility for your constituency,
with your promises at your election speeches
and your people;
you, brother,
you, sister,
you, man,
with all that money in your pocket?
Are we trying to be saviors to others?
Parents should be saviors to their children;
do you hear that?
Saviors.
Children should be saviors to their parents;
do you hear that?
Saviors,
especially when those parents are old;
husbands to their wives,
wives to their husbands,
brothers to sisters,
and sisters to brothers;
and if this really happens
and if this spreads,
then this world will change
because
all people
would be saviors
to all people;

and at that moment
all people would be Christ-like:
The kingdom has come.
Let us try.
Alleluia.
Amen.

43.

SIN AND COMMUNITY

From all the reports
that reached us
over all those centuries
from Jerusalem
and other places,
one thing seems to be fairly obvious:
    Once the followers of Jesus
    became aware of his Spirit in them,
    they immediately founded
    communities,
    and they lived together in a way
    they had never been living together before.
    His Spirit made them form ONE BODY.
There is for instance
that report on that kind
of relief service
to help the poor.
Foodstuffs, bread and fish and milk,
were handed out
to the widows and the poor.
But another thing is mentioned too;
irregularities slipped in:
    While the Greek widows,
    the minority,
    were queuing up at the front door,
    the Hebrew widows,
    the majority,
    were helped by their Hebrew friends
    at the back door.

Tribalism,
favoritism, brotherization,
and bribery
had crept in.
What slipped in can be called
by different names.
It can be named as well with a theological word:
SIN.
The new Spirit built a new community
and old favoritism,
sin,
broke it up.
    At the Department of Philosophy and Religious Studies
    I am obliged to read
    very many assignments,
    in fact too many,
    and quite a number of post-graduate dissertations.
    They often treat,
    directly and/or indirectly,
    ethical questions, that is,
    questions on how people should behave
    and how they should not behave
    according to all kinds
    of traditional African value systems.
    And those studies
    almost unanimously say
        that in the African traditional societies
        sin in the sense of offending God
        did not exist.
        If this is true,
        and I have no reason to doubt those statements,
        then it might help us
        to understand better
        what sin is.
Contrary to that African idea,
very many people seem to think
that sin means
to break a commandment of God.
And in fact

very many catechisms
say just that.
Those believers
will therefore confess,
very candidly,
"I have committed the sixth commandment,
ten times."
That of course means
that they had intercourse,
adulterously or fornication-wise,
which they consider
as against God's law,
illegal.
They therefore ask God
for forgiveness.
They offended God.
    Is that the only person they offended?
    Is that the only person they need forgiveness from?
    Is that the only other person involved?
Another will come,
and he says:
    "I stole.
    I disobeyed a command of God,
    I offended him,
    I ask him for forgiveness."
        Is that the only person offended?
        Is God really the person harmed?
        What about the damage done
        to the person he stole from?
In other words,
although I think
that we might say
that we offended God
and disobeyed his commandments,
we should as well
take something else into account.
    And that is a reality
    very well known in African societies:
    Sinful behavior

does not only offend God,
it does not even mainly offend God;
there is another more important aspect:
Sin
destroys our human community,
and
sin
destroys the sinner.
Sin is never something
that exists only between God and me.
It is something
that exists in me,
and in the community
where I sin.
    This can easily be seen
    in the context in which we live.
    Take the murdering of that member of parliament.
    It was bad
    not only because it offended God
    and cries out for his revenge.
    It is bad
    because it must have destroyed the murderer,
    and because it was so destructive
    to the community
    in which we live.
    It destroyed confidence,
    it broke down communications,
    it sowed hatred and suspicion,
    it originated all kinds of rumors,
    it cooled down the human temperature
    of the climate
    in which we have to live.
    It destroyed so much.
That is what sin does,
that is what sin does among us.
That is what sin did in Jerusalem.
They were building a community,
and favoritism broke it down,
helped it to blazes.

It is because of this destructive element
in sin
that God gave his commandments
as a guarantee
for our health and welfare.
That is what sin does,
and that is why
when we are asking for forgiveness,
we should not only turn to God.
The damage done
is not done to him as such.
The damage done
is done to ourselves
and to each other.
We should turn to each other, as well;
the thief to the person he stole from,
the abuser of others
to those abused.
We need to forgive each other,
and that is very difficult.
   We asked
   this morning,
   in the beginning of this celebration,
   for forgiveness of our sins.
   We heard his words:
   I forgive you all your sins.
But we should,
at that moment,
not only experience:
Now I am free.
   We should see it as well
   as a sacrament
   in which a power is given,
   the power
   to rebuild
   anew
   our human community
   and fellowship.

44.

THE HOLY,
WHOLE FAMILY

In 1938
a social worker in the United States
visited an isolated farm.
She found in the attic of that farm
a girl,
six years old.
The farm was run by the grandfather of the child.
She had been in that attic
since she was about five and a half months old.
Her name was ANNE.
She was an illegitimate child;
her grandfather did not want to see her
around the house.
Her mother happened to be of low intelligence,
and she was working
all day
on the farm.
    Anne had always been in that attic by herself.
    She had been living on cow milk.
    She was filthy and half-starved.
    She could not walk,
    she could not talk,
    she could not even express herself
    by gestures.
    She was brought to a children's home,
    and eighteen months later
    she was able to feed herself
    and walk.

Four years later
she started to talk,
just before she died
of a contagious disease.
Such a story
proves something
we all know.
A human being cannot
grow in isolation.
We need others,
we need a family to be able to grow up.
Anne, of course, had a family,
a mother,
a grandfather and a grandmother.
What really was missing
was human communication.
We need that communication with others.
It is that communication
that makes us grow.
In that communication with others:
    talking,
    singing,
    kissing,
    dancing,
    correcting,
    and praising,
    we form together
    a living bond,
    a living organism.
    We need to be with others.
If I bind my finger off
with a shoelace
in such a way
that the blood cannot pass
into my finger anymore,
then I cut the communication possibility
of my finger with the rest of the body.
There is no connection anymore.

And my finger will react.
It will turn all kinds of strange colors,
it will get darker and darker,
it will swell,
and turn green
and purple
and finally blue;
it is dying.
    If any part of my body escapes communication
    with the rest of my body,
    and if it starts
    to grow on its own
    without further control or contact,
    it forms a cancer in me.
    Such a cancer can be terminal.
    This terminal type of cancer,
    based on communication refusal
    or communication impotence,
    is a typical modern disease,
    a symbol of our times:
    lack of communication,
    isolation.
And even if we study
the troubles of human institutions,
like over here the University of Nairobi,
an institute called to form one community,
then everybody agrees
that the trouble is really
a lack of communication
between the old and the young,
between the staff and the students,
between the administration and the administered.
    Take all the troubles in the world;
    is it not at the moment
    that sound communication breaks down
    that revolutions are born,
    that Watergate affairs are developed,
    that mistresses have to jump out of senators' cars,

that the Middle East is in a mess,
and that the African Communities break up?
But let us go back to the family,
the holy family,
the whole family,
the family as a "whole,"
the family as one integrated unit.
   Our families should be
   living organisms,
   where children are conceived and born,
   where the mother is "expecting,"
   but where the father is "expecting" too.
   Where the child, once born,
   is taken up
   into the communication system
   that should exist between the father and the mother,
   between husband and wife.
   Where the child grows up
   in that communication system,
   learning for itself
   how to communicate
   lovingly
   in a holy family.
Husband and wife
should communicate
openly and frankly;
   how often do they not even know
   each other after years and years.
   Do you ever ask each other:
   What do you really think of this
   or of that,
   expecting to get
   his or her real answer?
This communication
means trust and confidence;
it does not exclude conflicts,
it knows about them,
and that knowledge,

that communication
is most probably already
part of the solution.
The doors of communication should always
remain open.
When those doors close,
life stops;
the family is not "holy" or "whole"
anymore.
Parents and children should communicate.
Children should be able to approach their parents
always on anything they want to.
If a child is not allowed to speak
to his parents,
then his parents
are no parents anymore.
They do not give life anymore;
they become functionaries,
hotel managers.
    But the bills
    will never be paid.
We should never forget
that the greatest gift
God gave humankind
is his SPIRIT.
And Spirit means
communication.

45.

NOT BEING ABLE TO COUNT UP TO SIX

Insofar as the Ten Commandments
are concerned,
it seems to be true
that very many people,
Christians and non-Christians,
are quite willing to count up to five,
but that they are not so willing
to count beyond that five.
They are willing to honor God,
they are willing to set a day apart for him,
and in honor of him for themselves,
as was foreseen;
they are willing to honor their father
and their mother;
they are willing to abstain from killing,
but then at that number six
an unwillingness seems
to creep in:
The temptation is too large,
the occasion too easy,
the price too cheap,
and the company quite respectable.
The company seems to be all right,
and the sin quite popular
among young and old.
That sixth commandment
is against fornication.

It is against fornication
in a certain context.
It is against fornication
in the context
of the conditions
necessary to build
a decent and bearable
human society.
A society in which people
would be allowed
to kill each other
would not be a livable society;
  a society in which people
  would be allowed
  to leave their parents
  to their fate
  would be an unbearable society;
and a society that would permit
fornication and adultery
without any further ado
would be an unbearable society as well.
  The Bible is not against sex.
  In fact the Bible is full of sex,
  ordered sex
  and unordered sex,
  recommended sex
  and forbidden sex.
Men and women
find each other
in the Bible
at waterwells
and in marketplaces,
behind trees
and in barns,
in orchards
and next to rivers,
in towns
and in villages.

In the Bible
people marry,
they have children,
they have sex in a full
and even overflowing measure,
in a measure that builds
the nation
and society.
But the Bible
is against
destructive sex.
It is against
that type of sex
    that destroys
    the human community,
    the human society,
    the human body of people.
The Bible is against
that type of sex
    that produces children
    without even the promise
    of a home,
    children that were never wanted
    or desired
    or provided for.
The Bible is against
that type of sex
    that breaks up
    the existing family relations,
    that undermines trust
    within the family,
    the trust and confidence
    that children need
    to grow up
    in security and peace.
The Bible is against
that type of sex
    in which boys

and girls
are used,
paid,
and abused.
The Bible is against
that type of sex
   that thrives
   on social inequality,
   on a dropout's problem,
   on economic poverty,
   on utter misery,
   on the hopelessness
   hidden under creams
   and powders,
   behind contraceptives
   and antibiotics.
The Bible is against
that type of sex
   that causes unfaithfulness,
   riots,
   arrests,
   distressed children,
   fights,
   and appearances in courts.
The Bible is against fornication,
Saint Paul is against fornication,
Pope Paul is against fornication,
the *Daily Nation* is against fornication,
   not because they are backward,
   old fashioned,
   or plain stupid,
   but because they wish us to be
   progressive,
   constructive,
   interested in the welfare of the people,
   in their persons,
   in their bodies,
   in the body of humankind.

That sixth commandment
that we should not fornicate
should not only be read in the negative.
There is the possibility of reading it in the positive.
The well-known American author
John Steinbeck,
a man well-known for his descriptions
of all kinds of fornication situations,
gave us,
in one of his books,
a hint
on how to read it
positively.
    When God,
        the maker of it all,
        the maker of us,
         our own cook,
         architect,
         and designer,
         told us,
            in smoke and in thunder,
            in lightning and in a cloud,
            with threats and admonitions,
            that we should not fornicate,
         he told us
         at the very same time
         that we should be able
         and that we in fact
         are able
         to live without it.
            He tells us
            that we are free,
            that we are not bound,
            that we are capable of organizing our lives,
            that that order is not beyond us,
            and it is that liberty
            that Saint Paul desires for us,
            and Pope Paul

and the editor of the *Daily Nation*
and all men and women of good will.
And it is that freedom
and liberty
that we should not only desire for each other
and for ourselves,
but it is the liberty and the freedom
we should realize together,
in view of a healthy,
        well-ordered,
        and constructive
        human and Christian community.

46.

A LAZY PROPHET
AND REPENTANCE

The first time
Jonah was called to go to Nineveh,
he took a world map,
he had a look at the position
of Nineveh,
he put a piece of cloth
over his face
to hide himself,
and he went to a travel agency
to buy a ticket
in the opposite direction,
to a town in Spain,
Tarshish,
a town that according to his map
was at the other end of the world,
as far from Nineveh as he could imagine.
    And you know the rest of the story,
    I suppose.
Once aboard
and on the sea,
a terrific storm started to surround the boat.
Enormous winds,
terrible gales,
threw the boat up and down.
The sailors became afraid
and then frightened,
they started to panic,

they called on all the gods they knew,
and it did not help.
They looked all over the boat,
whether there was perhaps a reason
or somebody
who might have called this storm over them.
And they found Jonah,
asleep,
and they shouted: Wake up;
they pulled him to his senses
and they said:
        You too,
            offer to your God.
A thing Jonah did,
but it did not help.
Then they tried to find out
who might be the cause of the calamity around them.
They cast lots
to find out,
and the lot fell on Jonah.
And they asked:
What did you do?
And Jonah said:
        It is not a question
        of what I did do.
        It is a question
        of what I did not do.
        And he told them
        how he was trying to run away from Yahweh.
And he suggested
they throw him overboard.
But they did not dare.
They first had another try.
        You do not throw
        a prophet
        overboard
        just like that.

They rowed and they toiled,
they sweated and they worked,
but it did not help.
And then they took Jonah
to throw him overboard
and he fell into the sea
imploring his God.
  And the sea became calm
  immediately,
  except for the movement
  of that big fish
  that swallowed Jonah,
  seated him in his belly,
  and then swam off,
  God's special delivery service,
  while Jonah,
  as he reported later,
  felt his heart faint in himself.
And the fish swam
in the correct
divinely indicated direction,
and it spat him out
at the entrance to the town of Nineveh.
  And it was then
  that Jonah got his second call
  and with seaweed in his hair,
  a salty taste in his mouth,
  water-bubbles singing in his ears,
  and a fish-smell all over
  he went into that big city.
He walked for one day,
and he said:
  You have only forty days more.
He walked a second day,
and he said:
  You have thirty-nine days more.
He walked a third day,
and he said:

You have thirty-eight days more
from now.
And then he went out of town,
and he took a room
in a motel,
to wait for what was going to happen,
to wait for the end.
An end that never came.
   That is to say
   the end did come.
   The intended,
   the divinely monitored end did come;
   but the end that Jonah expected
   never came.
Because the town converted,
and that was the end.
Even the king changed his ways;
he stepped from his throne,
he left his state house,
he changed his life,
and his ministers did the same
   and all people
   and all beasts
   and all herds
   and all flocks
   did not eat
   and they did not drink
   for quite some time
   to show that they wanted
   to change.
And therefore
the fire
and the earthquake
and the sulphur
and the smoke
and the broken arms
and the scorched legs
and the crushed necks

and the smashed skulls
  they never came.
  At least
  that is what Jonah thought
  and he got very angry.
  And he made a mistake,
  a mistake,
  lazy in his vocation
  and as lazy in his thinking.
Because his prophecy was fulfilled
after all.
Nineveh did change,
the old Nineveh was destroyed,
it did fall to pieces:
  There were no broken legs,
  but broken hearts;
  there were no crushed necks,
  but crushed consciences;
  there were not smashed skulls,
  but smashed pasts.
The old Nineveh passed away.
It passed away
in the same way
this world should pass away.
THIS WORLD
we know
should pass:
  It is no good,
  it definitely is not so very good;
  it should change,
  it should come to an end,
  not in the fire of God,
  not in the water of a flood,
  not in the earthquake of the end:
    We
    we
    we have to end it,
    we
    we

we heard the call,
we
we
we should not be lazy.
We should change.
It is very often said,
in these days
of charismatic upheavals and birth-pangs,
that such a change
can come,
with the power of God,
very suddenly,
in one blow,
in one stroke.
    That might be possible,
    it is possible.
    But in Nineveh it lasted forty days,
    and that is longer;
    it took some time,
    and forty in the Bible
    indicated quite some time.
    But during that period
    things,
    minds and hearts,
    changed.
Just like
in the period
that we are living,
1 x 40 or 2 x 40,
things should change,
slowly but consistently:
    listening to the commandments,
    following the example of Jesus,
    living according to those survival codes,
    and filling our heads,
                    minds,
                    and hearts
    with a new set of ideas
    and a new set of ideals.

47.

DO NOT FENCE ME IN

In Saint Paul's letter to Corinth
it is clear that something
had gone wrong.
The group was no longer one.
There was the group of Paul,
            the group of Apollos,
            the group of Peter,
            and the group of Christ.
Saint Paul sees only one solution,
that all return
to the group of Christ Jesus.
Then everything would be right again.
    Is that true?
    I doubt it.
    And I doubt it
    because I do not trust any group.
    I mistrust groups,
    and especially groups
    that are group-conscious.
    I do not like groups.
I am very upset,
every time
that someone tries to limit
or restrict me
to one group.
    I do not deny
    that I belong to groups;
    of course I belong to groups;
    how would I be able to survive

without the groups I belong to:
I belong to my family group,
I belong to my ethnic group,
the Taxandrians,*
I belong to my national group,
I belong to my church community.
But I do not want to be restricted to them.
If I say something
in the Department of Philosophy and Religious Studies
about a question,
let us say: abortion,
and somebody else would say:
 Of course,
 you have to think like that,
 because you are a Catholic,
 that is the official Catholic point of view,
then
I get very upset.
 I do not want to be restricted to a group;
 I belong to humankind,
 I belong to the world,
 I am taller and bigger,
 wider and more extensive
 than the largest and the biggest,
 the widest and the most extensive group.
 AND SO ARE YOU.
 Do not fence me in,
 do not put barbed wire all around me,
 do not pin me down to one place.
 Do not fence us in.
Out of very many conversations
and discussions with you,
I know
that all the ones among you

*The Germanic people inhabiting the author's home region in the
Netherlands.

who reflect,
and who among you does not reflect from time to time?
have that same idea
and that same kind of reaction.
 You can be very upset,
 if you are told by others:
 But that is what you,
 belonging to this or that group,
 are traditionally supposed to think.
 OR:
 Taking into consideration
 the religious denomination
 you belong to,
 you are supposed to . . . etc.
It seems that modern men and women,
like you and me,
do not feel fine
when they are restricted to the groups they belong to.
 Even not as a Christian.
 I am a Christian.
 I am a Catholic.
 But I am often very sad
 when other Christians restrict me to my Catholicism,
 or when non-Christians restrict me to my Christianity.
Not because I do not like
to belong to those communities.
But because I know what they mean to say.
They really mean to say
that I belong to a power group.
They want to say that I am dangerous,
because I am against them.
 Saint Paul invited the Corinthians
 to form one group.
 Most probably he wanted
 in that way as well
 to strengthen the influence
 of the Christians in Corinth.
 He wanted to unite them.

Very many people think
that if all Christians
would be united
in the world
through a successful ecumenical movement
that then Christianity would be unbeatable.
Christians of the world unite.
And they
very often
do not even hesitate to call the names
of the groups
we have to unite against.
I do not want to belong
to such a group.
I want to belong to a group
organized in the way
Christ organized his group,
and he organized his group
as he organized his own life.

    He had all power;
    in fact he said
    that he could call upon millions of angels
    to help him
    if he wanted to be helped.
    He did not use them.
    He came to serve,
    to serve all,
    to help all.
    In our Christian groups
    we very often do not follow that example.
    We ask,
    before we help,
    before we teach:
    Are you a Christian?
    Are you a Catholic?
All this is wrong;
it is not Christian,
it is not Jesus Christ.

Most of us know this
by now.
That is why I spoke about
our anti-group attitude
of modern men and women.
   As Christians we should help
   not ourselves
   to get into heaven;
   not our group
   to get into a power position;
   we should not even help
   in order to serve,
   but merely when and because our help is needed.
   And we should not only help.
   Helping is necessary
   because things are not yet well organized.
   We should as well reconstruct.
   And in this world
   no reconstruction can be based
   on a group,
   on one group only.
   Groups are out.
   Christ as Head should be in.

48.

CELEBRATING THE ANCESTORS

It is All Souls Day.
We are celebrating these days
our ancestors,
  the people whose blood is in us,
  the people whose past carries our present,
  the people whose words still vibrate in our minds.
  The people who died
  among us,
  the people who breathed their last breath
  among us,
  the people who have gone down,
  or did they go up?
  The people who were told by death
  to tie up their load and go,
  the people who had eaten enough
  among us,
  and who went home,
    sleeping forever and ever.
We celebrate all souls,
all spirits,
we are celebrating all the dead.
The dead, who according to African tradition
are not under the earth,
  but in the rustling trees,
      in the groaning woods,
      in the flowing water,
      in the thickening shadow,

in the moaning grass,
in the dark forest,
in the fire dying down.
In all human societies
the dead have been a problem.
Death is a problem,
but the dead too.
There are so many reports
of them appearing again.
Jesus himself reappeared so many times,
and at the very moment of his death
innumerable spirits rose from their tombs
and were roaming through town,
according to an authenticated report
that reached us from Jerusalem.
What do those dead people want from us?
Are they still hurting us?
Are we still hurting them?
Of course,
the dead can still be hurting us.
If a man kicked me in my teeth
before he died,
I am after his death
still with that broken tooth
of mine.
And if a man stole my money
before his death,
I am still without it
after his death,
and I think,
and quite a few people in the Christian community think,
that those who broke my tooth,
and those who stole my money,
and who are now dead
are not as happy as they could be
because of that.
Many think
that although finally saved

they might still be suffering
because they made us suffer,
and that suffering endures.
And that is where All Souls Day comes in;
we should pray for the dead,
we should pray for their happiness,
and that means
that we should be willing to forgive them,
all they did to us.
Because they too
fall under that saying of Christ:
First get straight with your community,
with your brothers and sisters.
They will get straight
when we pray for them
showing by that
our willingness to forgive them.
  Let us then pray for them,
  pray
  that they may be happy,
  and undisturbed,
  and with God.
But we too need,
in very many if not all cases,
forgiveness for all we did
to them.
Let us ask forgiveness from them.
And God will be with them
and with us;
he will bless our solidarity.
  Solidarity with the dead.
  Communion with the spirits.
  Communion with the Spirit of Jesus Christ.
  Did he not say
  that we should break his bread
  to commemorate him and his death
  until he comes,
  or until we come?

49.

THE JESUS-PRAYER

This story begins with a man
you all know,
that crippled man
sitting on top of the steps
in front of the City Market
at Muindi Mbingi Street,*
brought there every morning
by some of his relatives.
    That man has been sitting
    all through human history
    in all villages and in all towns
    of our human world.
    In Peter's time
    he was sitting in Jerusalem
    in front of the gate of Solomon.
    One morning Peter and John passed him.
    He asked for money.
    They had no money,
    but instead Peter told him the story of Jesus,
    and that story healed him.
Everybody was very surprised;
people gathered,
and they looked at Peter,
but Peter said to them:

*Site of a bustling market in Nairobi.

Do not look at me,
I did not do a thing;
it is the name of Jesus that did it.
They looked at John,
but John said to them:
Do not look at me,
I did not do a thing,
it is the name of Jesus that did it.
More and more people gathered,
their number rose to five thousand,
it grew into a demonstration,
the Temple Service Unit came into action,
they even sent a Captain to coordinate affairs,
people were arrested,
and next morning Peter and John
were standing in court,
and it is then
that Peter says:
For all the names given to man in the world
this is the only one
by which we can be saved.
And that only name was and is
JESUS.
A name that means:
a helper in need,
a savior,
a liberator,
a spacemaker.
And every time
that the name JESUS
is used in the New Testament,
that is what happens:
Help is given,
bonds are loosened,
space is made,
a light switches on
in the dark of this world.

Think of the blind,
who shouted: JESUS;
they were healed;
the deaf,
the dumb,
the stupid,
the hungry,
the thirsty,
the ignorant,
every time that name
JESUS
was uttered, whispered, or shouted by them:
    Help came down,
    help came up,
    space was created,
    liberty granted.
The power
of the name
JESUS.
    Some people are even convinced
    that the mere saying of the word JESUS
    still has that same redemptive effect.
    There is a whole school of mystics,
    and mystics are people
    who know more about divine realities
    than you or me,
    especially in that very old Christian country Russia,
    who have as their main spiritual exercise
    the saying of that name
    JESUS.
    The Jesus-prayer people.
    They say
    that if you say the name JESUS
    something happens to you,
    your mind widens,
    your attitudes improve,
    your charity becomes easier,
    you are going to go out to others,

you are going to help,
you are going to assist,
you are going to liberate,
you are going to pray.
By saying his name,
he grows in you.
It sounds mysterious,
but it is not so mysterious.
We all know that people become
what they say.
We all know that people
look like they talk.
Would you not be very surprised
if someone with a very noble and pious-looking face
suddenly would open the mouth in that face
and say something like,
with your permission,
shit.

  You become what you say.
  Did you ever hear that story
  told by that great Jewish philosopher Martin Buber.
  The story is about a lame old man,
  crippled completely
  just like the man
  in the beginning of this sermon.
  One day the grandson of that man
  asked him to tell a story.
  And he began to tell a story;
  he told the story about a very holy man,
  a man who was so holy
  that he could not sit still while he prayed;
  he always got so excited
  and so moved
  that he had to jump up
  and to dance.
  And while that old grandfather
  was telling that story
  he himself got so excited

that in order to demonstrate what he meant
he too jumped up
and started to dance.
He was healed from that moment.
Telling about dancing
made him dance again.
It is in this way
that those mystics,
those people of the Jesus-prayer,
and you find them as well in modern American literature,
in the books by Salinger for instance,
use the name of
JESUS.
It is in this way
that we should use the name of
JESUS,
    so that we, while pronouncing that name,
    oftener and oftener,
    become like him.
The only question that remains is not:
Does this type of prayer work?
It does.
The remaining question is,
Do we want to become like him,
like him
who is that shepherd
willing to lay down his life
for his flock?
    We very often say
    that we cannot pray.
    Nonsense.
    We should say
    that we do not dare to pray,
    because to pray means
    to become like him,
    and who wants to become
    like him?

50.

ADVENT OR UTOPIA

From all over this world,
people are coming to the city we live in,
to this city Nairobi,
to dream their dreams:
    Last year we had the World Bank,
    the International Monetary Fund;
    they spoke and dreamt about
    a more just division
    of the world's wealth.
      We had the meeting
      of the International Labor Organization,
      and although I wonder whether
      they were serious about it,
      they spoke and dreamt about
      work for everybody.
    There was the meeting
    about the neglected and handicapped children
    on this planet
    and plans were formulated to help,
    just in the same way they had been formulated
    in the conference on that problem
    the year before
    and the year before. . . .
Now the Christians are with us,
the World Council of Churches,
thousands of delegates,
to dream their dreams
about oneness and unity,
about open communion

and intercommunion,
about liberation
and common worship.
And their dreams even contain more than that.
It is not only about
the body and blood of Christ;
it is about
other realities
like a common cup of coffee.
Or like that South African delegate,
Dr. Manas Buthelezi, put it,
last Thursday:
 Why should we be thinking
 of sharing the blood of Christ,
 if we cannot share,
 in common,
  a cup of coffee?
And he knew what he was speaking about,
because he is not allowed,
in South Africa,
to drink a cup of coffee,
white or black,
together with a white man
in the same bar,
at the same table.
 Christians are not only dreaming
 about intercommunion
 and the forgiveness of sins,
 about peace of mind
 and conversion,
 about salvation
 and an inner light,
 they are dreaming about as well
a just world,
 in which people share,
 because they happen to be people;
a just world,
 in which there are no over-fed

and over-consuming nations
next to starving ones;
a just world,
    in which there are no rich people
    surrounded by dogs to protect them
    and poor people bitten by those dogs,
    losing their ears
    like Malchus;
a just world,
    in which there are no oppressors,
    and no oppressed people;
a world
    in which women,
            strangers,
            minority groups,
            and children
            are respected;
a world
    in which the shout "help"
    in the middle of the night
    is not heard any more,
    and if it is heard,
    people run out
    to protect the person
    who is threatened
    and not to profit from the occasion;
a world
    in which conversion
    has taken place;
a world
    in which people
    have turned to God
    and to each other;
a world
    in which peace of mind
    is acquired;
a world
    in which justice

rolls over the Ngong Hills
and over Mount Kenya,
over Mount Elgon
and the Kilimanjaro,
through the plains of Europe,
over the cities in the States,
and over the banana plantations
in South America.
    BUT OBVIOUSLY:
    We,
        they, are dreaming.
        Full of dreams,
        full of promises,
        like a beautiful virgin,
        full of dreams,
        full of promises.
And yet we know we are barren,
we know we are impotent,
it will never happen.
We will never bear those fruits;
it is a dream,
utopia,
and that means:
    Never and
    nowhere.
        Barrenness seems to be
        the lot of this world,
        the fate of this planet,
        the destiny of this generation.
        Some call it original sin.
That barrenness of this world
and of humankind
living in it,
has been described so very often
in all kinds of stories in the Bible.
    Think of Abraham's wife,
    Sarah.
    He,

and therefore she as well,
was living under the promise
of a whole generation,
of a people as numerous
as the stars.
But she,
she was barren,
as barren
as a piece of dry wood in the sun,
or was it he
who was so dry?
Think of Abraham's son Isaac
and his wife,
Rebecca.
She was so beautiful
and so full of promise
that Isaac could not believe his eyes,
nor his hands,
and yet she,
she was as barren as Sarah.
Or was it he
who was as barren
as his father?
  Think of Isaac's son
  Jacob
  and his wife,
  Rachel.
  When he saw her first
  his heart jumped up in his throat,
  and when she saw him,
  the same happened to her,
  but her womb remained empty.
All those wombs
remained empty,
until God intervened.
  Barrenness seems to be the lot of this world;
  the world is like that other barren woman
  in Holy Scripture:

Hannah,
    the wife of Elkanah,
    son of Jeroham,
    son of Elihu,
    son of Tohu,
    son of Zuph,
    an Ephraimite.
She,
barren,
went to the temple to pray,
and she prayed, prayed, prayed, prayed
to be allowed and able to give life.
She prayed for hours and hours,
day in day out;
she prayed so long
that she lost her voice
and could only whisper.
And then Eli saw her.
And he said:
    Go away, you are drunk;
but she said:
    I am not drunk, I am in trouble;
and he said:
    Get out, I do not believe you;
and she said:
    I did not pour in wine,
    I am pouring out my soul,
    I am asking for help.
Help in her barrenness,
help in the barrenness of this world,
so full of promise,
so full of dreams,
and yet so fruitless.
We should pray,
as Abraham and Sarah prayed,
as Isaac and Rebecca prayed,
as Jacob and Rachel prayed,
as Hannah and Elkanah prayed:

O Lord, raise up your might
and come.
And that is,
I am afraid,
a rather tame and lame translation,
made by monks in their celibate hours,
between vespers and compline.
The prayer really says:
    O Lord, excite your potency;
     give us life.
But that is not the end
of this sermon,
because it is not the end of the story:
    That prayer is heard, that prayer was heard,
    that prayer has been heard:
    The power is given already;
    we are,
    as Saint Paul wrote,
    not without it;
    we have the Spirit,
    we should bring forth its fruits
    and then
    utopia will turn into advent:
    the coming of the Lord.

51.

A CITY AS THE ANSWER

Saint John describes
the final outcome of our human history
as the founding of a town,
descending from heaven,
a holy town,
a huge city,
built up with gold and precious stones,
with a river in the middle
and no tears,
with all the people and
    without hospitals,
    without clinics,
    without schools,
    without social services,
    without mortuaries.
According to his vision
one day
the whole of humankind
will be collected in that town.
Maybe we,
over here in the city of Nairobi,
are not so very impressed,
because we live in a town,
even in one of the nicer ones
in the world.
    But for the rural
    up-country people,
    this image,
    this ideal,

corresponds to one of their greatest desires
and wishes:
    to go to town,
    to end up in town.
Is not every up-country youth
in this country
dreaming of going
downtown?
    Trains and buses are full of them each day.
They are convinced that things happen in town,
that human life in town
is in a higher gear
than in their villages.
They come to town,
and they try to look like townspeople.
The girls from up-country
do not like for everybody to see
that they have been working in the sun up-country
and that they got so sunburned.
They try to get rid of that sunburned look
with bleaching creams,
with bu-tone and ambi,
with snow-fire.*
They even try to lose the smell
of their location,
that smell of earth
and dung
and the woodfires.
They wash themselves with perfumed soap,
and they dab some smell behind their ears
from bottles
sold at the bus stops.
Town has a terrific attraction.
When you are up-country
and you say that you are coming
from town,

*Brand names of skin toners.

people will look at you
as if you are a miracle:
   So you LEFT the place,
   they always loved to go to.
And that is not only true in Kenya.
Did you ever meet an American
who admitted coming from a village?
They all come from New York
or from Boston or Denver,
Chicago or Los Angeles.
I wonder who is living up-country in the States.
   Jesus felt that attraction too.
   Matthew wrote how they went to live
   in the city of Nazareth.
   But Nathanael would say later:
   Nazareth, that up-country village?
   And Jesus,
   that up-country man,
   went afterwards to the great city of Jerusalem.
   He stated
   that a prophet
   should die
   in or near
   a city.
   He had tears in his eyes
   when he saw town.
   He compared himself and his disciples
   with a town
   in the full light
   on the top of a mountain.
   Jesus longed for a town,
   and John said,
   It is a town
   we are going to get,
   a beautiful large town.
To some of us
that desire for a city,
that desire for a place

where all people will be together
might seem rather frightening.
Too many of us have been living in a large town,
too many of us know about the disadvantages:
    Town is smelly,
    town is cruel to many,
    town is lonely,
    town is lacking in humanity,
    town is lacking in divinity.
Saint Peter knew about town
he was going to be arrested
and to be murdered in one of them.
Saint Paul knew about town;
he was imprisoned
and beaten up in several of them.
John knew about town;
he addressed seven of them
on their vices
and sins,
    and yet according to him,
    the final outcome
    would be a city,
    a holy city.
When we speak about holy cities,
about Rome
or Mecca
or Benares,
we think about their temples,
their churches,
their sacred shrines and places of worship.
But of that final city
Saint John says:
There is no temple.
The people there
do not need those things any more,
because God is with them always.
    They have not to come together,
    like we do

this morning,
to be with God at a special hour
on a special day.
They do not need to come together
to eat their bread
together,
like we do
this morning.
What we do
this morning
in this chapel
around Christ
for about fifty minutes
will be there
the common practice.
And it is not the common practice
with us, as yet.
Eating our bread together
over here in this chapel
this morning
means
that we manage to do something
we do not as yet manage
in our daily life.
   This morning
   in this chapel
   there are members of families together,
   sharing the bread of Jesus
   who would not be able to eat together
   at the same time
   and at the same table,
   except over here
   eucharistically.
There are here
this morning
in this chapel
representatives of peoples
that hardly ever would risk
being seen together

or eating together.
   There are here
   this morning
   in this chapel
   old people
   and young people
   who understand each other
   only when they are together over here.
We are not yet fulfilled,
we are not yet together,
we are still split over
   generations,
   races,
   tribes,
   peoples,
   classes,
   and salary groups.
We need a temple,
we need his table,
we need his bread,
we need his spirit.
   But finally
   in that heavenly city
   we do not need a temple,
   we do not need his table,
   we do not need his bread,
   but in his spirit
   we will be able to be with God
   and to be with each other.
   We will be together,
   all of us,
   and always
   in that heavenly city
      because we are trying now
      this morning
      in this chapel
      to be as near
      to that new Jerusalem
      as possible.

52

WHAT ARE WE
WAITING FOR?

Before he left,
Jesus asked his disciples
to wait,
to wait in Jerusalem
for the Spirit
he was going to send them.
    And his disciples waited,
    and I have the impression,
    when I look around,
    that his disciples
    are still waiting.
We are all waiting,
we are all saying:
    It cannot go on in this way;
    something has to happen,
    something is bound to happen,
    things cannot possibly stay as they are;
    it is too bad,
    everything should change.
That is how Christians talk about their church,
priests about their bishops
and bishops about their priests;
parents about their children
and children about their parents;
students about the administration,
the administration about the government,
the government about the international situation,
and so on.

It is even the way
in which we speak about ourselves.
We say that we are going to stop smoking,
but not today,
tomorrow.
We say that we are going to stop fornicating,
but not tonight,
tomorrow night.
We say that we are going to study efficiently,
really efficiently,
next week,
and we wait,
we wait
like the two men
in the play by Samuel Beckett.
They were waiting for Godot,
and that means a small god,
and they wait,
and wait;
all their hope is grounded
on Godot coming,
he is going to change everything;
but he does not come
and in the end
they say to each other,
let us go,
but they do not go.
They go on waiting,
although they know
that it must be in vain.
We wait,
as a matter of fact
our whole life is waiting:
We are waiting to finish our studies,
we are waiting for graduation day,
we are waiting to be loved,
we are waiting for our money,
we are waiting to be able to buy a new pair of shoes,

we are waiting for a letter from home,
we are waiting for the outcome of the discussions
    on the national service,
we are waiting for children,
we are waiting to be healed,
and in the end we are waiting for death.
We are waiting all the time.
But all those things
are not the real things we are waiting for.
The end of my studies
will not be the end of my waiting.
The letter from home
will not be the end of my waiting.
Even the coming of my child
will not be the end of my waiting.
Those things are not even
the beginning
of the end
of my waiting.
   What we are really waiting for
   lies much deeper.
   The real thing we are waiting for
   is infinitely more
   than all the things mentioned
   or all the things
   that we might mention.
   Our waiting goes deeper:
      We are waiting
      for the dark and the incomprehensible
      in our lives
      to be cleared up.
      We are waiting for answers
      to questions like these:
      Why the good are murdered,
      and why the murderers are never found;
      why there is suffering
      and war,
      conflict, and strife;
      why there is ignominy

and corruption,
starvation and bribery,
why there is so little respect,
and why nothing is done;
why things seem to turn bad
and sour
all the time, again and again,
and why nobody is doing
anything about it.
We are waiting for the force
and the power
to come
and to change all that.
We are all wrong.
We are waiting as if nothing happened
already.
We are praying with the old psalmist
to God:
    "From the depths
    I am shouting, O GOD,
    why are you not coming to my rescue?"
as if God did not come as yet.
We are still praying like the old Luyia:*
    "Po, God may the day dawn well,
    may you spit upon us
    your medicine
    so that we may walk well."
Or like the old woman Mukambi
in Ngugi's book *The Fig Tree*:
    "O Murungu, God of Gikuyu and Mumbi,
    who dwells on high Kirinyaga,
    yet is everywhere,
    why do you not release me
    from my misery?"†

* The Luyia people are an important Bantu group in western Kenya.

†Ngugi wa Thiongo is the best known Kenyan author. "Murungu" is an old Gikuyu name for God. The Gikuyu are the most numerous people in Kenya. "Mumbi" is their ancestral mother. "Kirinyaga" is the Gikuyu name for Mount Kenya.

We are often praying
and waiting
as if he did not yet come.
We are still waiting for a God,
who sent his son.
We are still waiting for his son,
who came two thousand years ago,
and who sent us their Spirit.
We are still waiting for that Spirit,
forgetting
that he was given to us,
very long ago.
He is within us.
    We are waiting for a reality
    that in reality
    came already.
    We are waiting for the bread
    we ate;
    for the life
    we got;
    for the power
    we obtained;
    for the force
    we received.
        We are waiting to catch the fish
        that is already caught;
        we are waiting to light the candle
        that is already lit;
        we are waiting for a life
        that is already born.
We do not believe;
we are waiting because we do not believe.
We are waiting for ourselves;
everything is given already,
everything is within
and with us.
    AMEN
    ALLELUIA

Other Orbis Titles

GOD, WHERE ARE YOU?

by Carlos Mesters

Meditations and reflections on significant figures and events in the Bible. "We shall," says Mesters, "try to restore to the word of God the function that it ought to have: to serve as a light on the pathway of life, as a help to our own understanding of present-day reality in all its complexity."

ISBN 0-88344-162-4 CIP   *Cloth $6.95*

THE EXPERIENCE OF GOD

by Charles Magsam

"His range is comprehensive; his orientation is personal, biblical, communitarian; his tone is positive and encouraging: all in all, a one-volume course on how to be free wholesomely for God, for oneself and for others." *Prairie Messenger*

ISBN 0-88344-123-3   *Cloth $7.95*
ISBN 0-88344-124-1   *Paper $4.95*

JESUS OF NAZARETH

Meditations on His Humanity

by Jose Comblin

"St. Teresa of Avila warned her nuns to beware of any kind of prayer that would seek to eliminate all reference to the human aspect of Christ. I think Jose Comblin would agree that her warning also describes the theme of his extremely valuable book that can be read and re-read many times with great benefit." *Priests USA*

ISBN 0-88344-231-0   *Cloth $5.95*

PRAYER AT THE HEART OF LIFE

by Brother Pierre-Yves Emery

"Emery's approach is both realistic and down-to-earth and profound and moving. This book can be recommended to anyone interested in a practical analysis of prayer, particularly the specific relationship between prayer and life itself." *Review for Religious*

ISBN 0-88344-393-7

Cloth $4.95

PILGRIMAGE TO NOW/HERE

by Frederick Franck

"Every now and then a true gem of a book appears that fails to get caught up in the tide of promotion, reviews, and sales, and, despite its considerable merits, seems to disappear. Such a book is Dr. Frederick Franck's *Pilgrimage to Now/Here*. His *Zen of Seeing* has been a steady seller, and *The Book of Angelus Silesius* is moving well. What happened to *Pilgrimage*, which in many ways is a more important book? Since Orbis is known as a religious publishing house, many distributors and booksellers are reluctant to stock it. Yet this is a religious book in the most significant sense of that word—in what Frederick Franck would call the search for meaning—for it is an account of a modern pilgrimage by jet, bus, train, and on foot to visit holy places and meet Buddhist leaders and Zen masters in India, Ceylon, Hong Kong and Japan."

East West Journal

ISBN 0-88344-387-2

Illustrated Paper $3.95

BIBLICAL REVELATION
AND AFRICAN BELIEFS

edited by Kwesi Dickson and Paul Ellingworth

"Essays by scholars who are themselves both African and Christian and who share a concern that Christian theology and African thought be related to each other in a responsible and creative way. There is no comparable book; this one should be in any library attempting serious coverage of either African thought or Christian theology." *Choice*

ISBN 0-88344-033-4

Cloth $5.95

ISBN 0-88344-034-2

Paper $3.45

IN SEARCH OF THE BEYOND

by Carlo Carretto

"The book describes an 'aloneness' that draws hearts closer to-gether, a 'withdrawal' that enriches family and community ties, a love of God that deepens human love." *America*

ISBN 0-88344-208-6   *Cloth $5.95*

LETTERS FROM THE DESERT

by Carlo Carretto

"It has been translated into Spanish, French, German, Por-tuguese, Arabic, Japanese, Czech, and now, gracefully enough (from Italian) into English. I hope it goes into twenty-four more editions. It breathes with life, with fresh insights, with wisdom, with love." *The Thomist*

ISBN 0-88344-279-5   *Cloth $4.95*

THE GOD WHO COMES

by Carlo Carretto

"This is a meaty book which supplies on every page matter for reflection and a spur to the laggard or wayward spirit. It offers true Christian perspective." *Our Sunday Visitor*

ISBN 0-88344-164-0   *Cloth $4.95*

FREEDOM TO BE FREE

By Arturo Paoli

"Full of eye-opening reflections on how Jesus liberated man through poverty, the Cross, the Eucharist and prayer." *America*

ISBN 0-88344-143-8   *Paper $4.95*

SILENT PILGRIMAGE TO GOD

The Spirituality of Charles de Foucauld

by a Little Brother of Jesus
preface by Rene Voillaume

"Sets out the main lines of Charles de Foucauld's spirituality and offers selections from his writings." *America*

ISBN 0-88344-459-3   *Cloth $4.95*

AFRICAN TRADITIONAL RELIGION: A DEFINITION

by E. Bolaji Idowu

"This important book is the first to place the study of African religion in the larger context of religious studies. . . . It includes an index and notes. There is no comparable work; this one should be in any collection on African religion." *Choice*

ISBN 0-88344-005-9   *Cloth $6.95*

THE PATRIOT'S BIBLE

edited by John Eagleson and Philip Scharper

"Following the terms of the Declaration of Independence and the U.S. Constitution, this faithful paperback relates quotes from the Bible and from past and present Americans 'to advance the kingdom and further our unfinished revolution.' " *A.D.*

ISBN 0-88344-377-5   *Paper $3.95*

THE RADICAL BIBLE

adapted by John Eagleson and Philip Scharper

"I know no book of meditations I could recommend with more confidence to learned and unlearned alike." *St. Anthony Messenger*

ISBN 0-88344-425-9   *Cloth $3.95*
ISBN 0-88344-426-7   *Pocketsize, paper $1.95*

UGANDA: THE ASIAN EXILES

by Thomas and Margaret B. Melady

"Takes its inspiration from the announcement in August 1972 by General Idi Amin Dada, President of Uganda, that he was told in a dream to order the expulsion of all Asians from Uganda. Tom and Margaret Melady were there and were witness to the tragic events. The book surveys the gruesome events following the expulsion order and the irrational pattern of Amin's record as well as providing a factual background of the Asian presence in Africa. The historical, economic and social complexity of the African-Asian-European situation in Uganda is made clear. Stories of personal devotion and heroism put flesh on the facts." *Religious Media Today*

ISBN 0-88344-506-9 CIP   *Cloth $6.95*

TANZANIA AND NYERERE

A Study of Ujamaa and Nationhood

by William R. Duggan and John R. Civille

"Sympathetic survey of Tanzania's attempt to develop economically on an independent path." *A Journal of World Affairs*

ISBN 0-88344-475-5 CIP
Cloth $10.95

RHODESIA: THE STRUGGLE FOR FREEDOM

by Leonard Kapungu

"A moving account of black Rhodesia's struggle for racial equality. It is a grim story, told by one who has lived it, with an equally grim conclusion." *America*

ISBN 0-88344-435-6
Cloth $5.95

BURUNDI: THE TRAGIC YEARS

by Thomas P. Melady

"Melady offers an eyewitness account of the tragic events in Burundi from April through August 1972, during which time as many as one hundred fifty thousand people died and a half million more were made homeless." *Journal of Church and State*

ISBN 0-88344-045-8
Cloth $4.95

POLYGAMY RECONSIDERED

by Eugene Hillman

"This is by all odds the most careful consideration of polygamy and the attitude of Christian Churches toward it that it has been my privilege to see." *Missiology*

ISBN 0-88344-391-0
ISBN 0-88344-392-9
Cloth $15.00
Paper $7.95